PoVo

PoVo

Edited by

Adam Novaldy Anderson

First published in 2024 by
Sweatshop Literacy Movement Inc.
ACE (Arts & Cultural Exchange)
8 Victoria Road, Parramatta NSW 2150,
Australia

www.sweatshop.ws

Printed and bound by Ligare Book Printers
Distributed by NewSouth Books

A catalogue record for this book is available
from the National Library of Australia

ISBN 978-0-6457179-0-7 (paperback)
ISBN 978-0-6457179-1-4 (ebook)

Design and typesetting by Duane Leewai 2024

Sweatshop Literacy Movement
acknowledges the Traditional
Custodians of Country throughout
Australia and their connections to
lands, waters and communities. We
pay our respect to Elders past and
present and extend that respect
to all Aboriginal and Torres Strait
Islander peoples today. We honour
more than sixty thousand years of
storytelling, art and culture.

Acknowledgements

Sweatshop Literacy Movement is proudly supported by ACE (Arts & Cultural Exchange), DARTS (Diversity Arts Australia) and the Australia Council, its arts funding and advisory body.

The contents of this publication have been developed in partnership with the Asylum Seekers Centre and Campbelltown City Council as part of the Campbelltown Youth Literacy Initiative.

Production Team

Editor: Adam Novaldy Anderson

Project Manager: Winnie Dunn

Commissioning Editor: Sara M. Saleh

Copy Editor: Michael Mohammed Ahmad

Proofreaders: Patrick Cruz Forrest and Yasir Elgamil

Design and Typesetting: Duane Leewai

Special Thanks: Lena Nahlous, Diana Chamma, Paula Pfoeffer, Dom Ellis, Danielle Townsend and Anne Loxley

Table of Contents

GUTTER

CRUMBS

Introduction

Adam Novaldy Anderson

During a shift at a certain fast food restaurant (let's call it Scamm'd), I was people-watching from the open kitchen. I noticed that the number of Anglo and Asian couples eating at the faux picnic tables was well into the double digits. The Sydney CBD location was pumping on a Friday night. Collared shirt yuppies downed twelve-dollar Coronas and rich Chinese travellers were sampling the exotic Western cuisine.

I pointed out the couples to another worker — a fellow Indonesian whose curly hair suggested he was from an Eastern Island — and asked him for his opinion on why this was so common. I suggested romantic racism and the emasculation of Asian men, which made us less desirable than men from other cultural backgrounds.

Before I finished my out-loud pondering, my co-worker paused his deep-frying, turned to me and rubbed his upturned finger and thumb together — making the money gesture so vigorously it might have ignited a little fire. I dismissed it as an oversimplification and went back to the eye-stinging work of running the char-grill. However, I have to admit, his succinct, wordless analysis was more accurate than mine.

In her essay collection *Writing Beyond Race*, bell hooks introduces us to the term 'imperialist White supremacist capitalist patriarchy'. This concept identifies the interlocking systems of colonial, racialised, economic and gendered hierarchies that exist across the globe and how they 'work together to uphold and maintain cultures of domination'. Back at the fast food restaurant, the 'ethnics' in these relationships weren't just dating 'White people', they seemed to be stepping through the door to a higher social class. At least, that must have been the plan.

Years later, I came across the works of Indonesian novelist, historian and political prisoner, Pramoedya Ananta Toer. In the four novels that comprise his *Buru Quartet*, a similar dynamic can be observed in the character Nyai Ontosoroh, aka Sanikem. Set in the Dutch East Indies at the turn of the century, Nyai's father — assistant to a cruel colonial administrator — married his daughter off to a Dutch entrepreneur. He gloated to his wife, 'Sanikem is now richer than the Queen of Solo', not knowing that the Dutchman was, in fact, a failure. Nyai's father was unaware that the Dutchman had fled for Holland after legally dispossessing Nyai of the land and business she had worked her entire life to make profitable, as well as the custody of her own daughter.

Reading this, I sensed an obscure connection to the story of my own parents, whose international–intercultural relationship carried class expectations that didn't manifest in the way either had expected. Dad — the eldest child of a working-class, White, convict-settler family in Gosford — worked as a carpenter. In 1990, he had saved enough to afford an international boat trip to France with a layover in Indonesia. Mum was a hotel housekeeper when she met Dad in a Yogyakarta nightclub.

Dad never made it to France. After a few dates, Mum returned to the kampung with news that an Australian man had proposed to her. My grandparents — conservative Muslims who had only ever left Indonesia for Hajj — were confused. *What was this bule doing in Java? Why did he choose their eldest daughter?* However, the economic opportunity in Australia was too great to pass up. Wanting the best for their grandchildren, they accepted his proposal.

When Mum arrived in Australia, it wasn't the 'Diamond Life' she had imagined it would be. To make ends meet, she started a childcare centre from the back of our three-bedroom house in Tamworth — a business which she runs to this day.

My parents eked out a comfortable, middle-class lifestyle for me and my brothers. We had plenty of food, a computer with internet, two cars, and a holiday each year. On the occasions we returned to Indonesia, my eldest aunty would line up my cousins and instruct me to give them each the same amount of red 100,000-rupiah bills. This would create extra family time, as no one needed to pester me to buy them this or that, or squabble over who gets what. But no matter what strategies my aunty used, resentment and envy seemed inevitable. My uncle still made comments about how freely my dad's family spent money and my three teenage cousins gasped at the cost of my sunglasses.

———

In 2021, the World Economic Forum announced that the poorest half of the global population owned just 2% of the global wealth, while the richest 10% owned 76% of all wealth. Our current economic system uses the practice of artificial scarcity (having capacity to produce enough for everyone but restricting access to products for profit) and spreads an ideology of individualism (the idea that opportunity is equal and people arrive at their achievements through hard work alone). As a result, we get a society where community connection and solidarity are replaced by a violent mess of competing needs.

Capitalism produces disconnected bands of suspicious humans, afraid to help each other for fear of losing their own share. Sometimes, I have days where my only interaction with the community is someone giving me the middle finger out a car window or catching a sour whiff of the guy with the dog that sits outside Bankstown TAB.

Late capitalism has led us to a period in history fraught with economic and existential crisis. This generation is likely to be the first in Australia's history not to do as well as their parents: a 2019 report by the Grattan Institute found that 'economic pressures on the young have been exacerbated by recent wage stagnation and rising under-employment', concluding that 'living standards have improved far less for younger Australians'.

———

While collecting cooking oil from my unused mie goreng bumbu sachets, I had the uplifting privilege of working with Sweatshop's incredible community of First Nations and culturally and linguistically diverse writers. Together we produced *Povo*, a new anthology devoted to empowering marginalised writers from low socio-economic status. Through stories that reflect their own experiences, these writers resist the White-dominated Australian literary community and the classism which plagues literature down to its flowery purple prose; the kind people generally associate with the idea of 'good writing'.

Kicking off the anthology is Indigenous-Tongan writer, Forever Tupou, with a debut short story that left me awe-struck. In her writing, the present effect of colonial history pervades almost every sentence; examining the social influence of hardcore Christianity, alcohol's ever-present role in the colony, the domination of patriarchy, and the problem of gambling — all in simple, direct and detail-packed prose that elegantly depicts the complexities of her community and relationships.

Like Tupou's piece, many of the stories in this collection revolve around accommodation and property — an appropriate theme for a country experiencing an ever-worsening housing crisis. In August 2023, *The Guardian* revealed a report that found 1,600 Australians are pushed into homelessness each month. Many of the stories in *Povo* mimic these findings. Yasir Elgamil calls out Australia's poor housing standards with a grim sense of humour. Victor Guan Yi Zhou gets down and out in Sydney's north side — his character forced to choose between his aspirations and his identity. Rayann Bekdache chronicles the misfortunes of a woman who fights to protect her own space and time.

Out on the streets, Daniel Nour, Adrian Mouhajer and Natalia Figueroa Barroso write stories about cars — machines that act as visual signs of our current economic conditions and extensions of our identities. This is especially true in Western Sydney; a city that hums and growls with engines. Lines of brake lights snaking beyond the horizon; a WRX or a Skyline or an Evo are the key to standing out. Some blast their exhaust with custom bodywork and surfboard-sized spoilers. Others prefer to prove their individuality surreptitiously; literally getting ahead in their high-performing vehicles — anything to stick out from the tradies in their trucks and HiLuxes, broke boys in the backseats of the family Tarago or, god forbid, the poor souls riding the bus.

Accompanying houses and cars in this book is the theme of labour. Meyrnah Khodr subverts the myth of meritocracy with a working-class tale of loyalty and tragedy. In contrast, Helen Nguyen reveals the downside to upward social mobility; expressed by a story of guilt and longing for the people and experiences she's had to leave behind.

Palestinian-Australian writer, Katie Shammas; Afro-Brazilian-Australian writer, Guido Melo; and Ghanaian-Australian poet, Jessicca Wendy Mensah contribute pieces that describe poverty as the force behind migration — linking the colonialism of the past with the poverty of today. Each of these pieces offers a new perspective on the journeys so many of us have made and continue to make throughout Australia: leaving the place and community where all our connections and familiarities lie to take a chance on an unknown future — language and memory the only tools left in the struggle to survive.

Alongside the contributions of these 'Sweatshop Writers', this publication is also gifted with the stories of newly arrived Australian storytellers. In May 2023, Sweatshop collaborated with the Asylum Seekers Centre — a Sydney-based organisation that provides support services, community engagement and legal advocacy for people seeking asylum in Australia.

Sweatshop General Manager, Winnie Dunn and I were fortunate to sit down with four incredible people — Khaled Elkady, Arash X, Sangee X and Thouraya Lahmadi — and collaborate with them to commit their stories to writing. We called the result *Fences*: a series of stories that range from heart-warming affection to unimaginable horror, each delivered in the distinctive, idiosyncratic voice of a writer still learning to navigate, among many other things, the English language.

I was also honoured to receive contributions that were commissioned and edited by award-winning author, activist and human rights lawyer, Sara M. Saleh. The collection — titled *Crumbs* — features five unique and incisive voices who write from diverse communities across Greater Sydney: Leila Mansour, Jenanne Ibrahim, Fahad Ali, Priyanka Bromhead and Nadia Demas. As a daughter of migrants from Palestine, Egypt and Lebanon, I could think of no one better than Sara to curate stories from such an eclectic array of emerging and established writers.

Further contributions include two collections of throw-ups we produced in partnership with Campbelltown City Council during workshops in Western Sydney high schools. The first collection is written by students of Leumeah High School. Labelled *Eshays*, these pieces are overflowing with teenage rage, love and anxiety as they struggle to discover their identity, endure migration and find their place in the world.

The second collection is from Macquarie Fields High School. Titled *Gutter*, these pieces remain untitled and anonymous due to the dangerous and illicit worlds that their all-too-young writers find themselves in. What's interesting here is that class is not only the subject of these stories, it's the style — each word loaded with the broad spectrum of socio-economic conditions throughout Western Sydney.

The final piece in *Povo* is by Kuku Djungan, Muluridji, Wakaman, Tagalaka, Kunjen, Warrgamay and Yindinji writer and actor: Phoebe Grainer. Her story depicts the dust and deprivation that drives young people away from country towns — the material realities that displace Indigenous youth from their families and communities. This compounds with the ongoing colonial violence that disconnects Indigenous people from Country. Writing from the less vocal side of Australia's city–country divide, Phoebe's writing acts as a counterpoint to Forever Tupou's opening depiction of urban poverty.

Addressing socio-economic difference in First Nations communities is of utmost importance when poverty continues to push young Indigenous people into a carceral justice system which has again and again proven lethal. Aboriginal deaths in custody are beyond measure; a terrible, ongoing horror that continues to plague and shame our country. This anthology is book-ended by two First Nations writers because it has been created on land that always was and always will be.

The stories in *Povo* are overflowing with the histories of nations, struggles for identity, family drama, unlikely triumph and profound tragedy. My hope for this anthology, like so many of our emotions, can be related to an aphorism once written by James Baldwin: 'You think your pain and your heartbreak are unprecedented in the history of the world, but then you read.' I hope this book falls into readers' hands at their loneliest of moments. Perhaps on break from a job they loathe having to do. Maybe hiding out at a library because they can't afford to heat or cool their home. Or stranded on a platform waiting for a train that may or may not come. I hope this book inspires people of low socio-economic backgrounds to see past class barriers and feel entitled to a safe and prosperous future. There's enough for everyone; as long as we dismantle the imperialist White supremacist capitalist patriarchy that tells us otherwise.

Francis Street
Forever Tupou

Every time my mum made that right turn in our 1980 Mazda 363 — 'Red Betty' — off Livingstone Road onto Francis Street in Marrickville, I would cover my seat belt buckle with two hands, two hundred metres from my dad's boarding house. Standing on the road, barefoot, ready to peel me out of the back left side of the car, my stowaway, menace to Australian society, Christian, gay-basher dad — who played pokies and ran in marathons to win — took me into his custody and my mum shot off down the hill and turned left or right depending on where she was going to smoke a Winnie Blue and feel like herself again. I screamed my guts out of my face. Anyone who heard the sound wondered how it got there and became disturbed. At the bottom of the hill, the backs of Vietnamese restaurants confirmed I wasn't at our leafy, freshly painted Beauchamp Street housing commission safe haven, I was at the Francis Street nut house.

Fat Maria sat on one of several miscellaneous hand-me-down chairs on the front porch next to the 'Rooms To Let' sign for hours, her welcoming face promoting Francis Street and all it had to offer, until she would disappear into one of the two toilets in the backyard and fill it to the brim with her shit. The front of the house was south-facing and presented in its own shade. Below the porch, on top of concrete, two shallow, rectangle garden beds made from brick cut offs, with rocks and cigarette butts for soil, homed two blue hydrangea flower bushes that smelled like the stale scent of the house. The distinct smell travelled across the tattered carpet hallway via the draft from the concrete backyard; crossed the grass patch, red and yellow bins and a haggard silver Hills Hoist; through the sooty shared kitchen and small bathroom in the corner, then drifted past ten closed doors and out the front one that stayed open at night, spilling out and around the side of the house.

Thirteen Francis Street was around the corner from Marrickville RSL Club which looked like a Las Vegas casino on the inside and Marrickville train station that had two railway lines — City Circle and the Bankstown line. Across the tracks was McNeilly Park that had an abandoned pool from the 80's — a place where Viet gangs had quick knife fights, Fobs had all-nighter drink ups and Lebanese gangs occasionally fired shots. On the corner of Illawarra Road next to the station was Marrickville Centrelink; the place of standing and waiting in line for hours with no context like Fat Maria on the front porch. We were surrounded by a pentagon of churches: St Nicholas Greek Orthodox, St Brigid's Catholic, Marrickville Road Anglican, Marrickville Baptist and Marrickville Uniting.

Dad strolled around the Liquor Land with his disguised sack, a white long-sleeved top with a knot tied at the bottom draped over his forearm like a butler, quietly slipping in bottles of spirits. Doink. Doink. His regular buyer was at the old, hole-in-the-wall, Greek shoe repair shop on Illawarra Road opposite the Woolworths. He exchanged the bottles for yellow and red notes and I sniffed the shoe polish. We lined up at the churches for free food packages and caught the bus or train into Central Station to eat at the food trucks for the homeless. Dad would hide under cars and jump into trees if he saw a cop and pretend to be asleep when a ticket officer approached. He often gave away our money and made sure to prove a point that we could survive on nothing as long as God was with us. We shared a thirty-cent soft serve inside a ten-cent bread roll from the Vietnamese bakery.

In the backyard, we stretched on the concrete in the sun for counts of fifteen and did sit-ups up to fifty after our runs around the neighbourhood and ten uphill sprints. He was building me up for greatness, training me for the Olympics. He talked about God and plucking my eyes out until

I wanted to pluck my own eyes out. I enjoyed his post-run fried egg and salad sandwiches pressed together with love and cut in half by his violent hands. When I had nosebleeds I squinted up at the sky, blood dripping down the back of my throat.

Dad cooked dark purple chicken hearts and chewy ox tongue from the Asian butcher on top of the dirty stove in the kitchen and sprinkled salt from a seven-hundred-and-fifty gram Saxa red and white salt shaker. We collected rainwater in white buckets and boiled it in the communal jug to drink God's gift. Once I dropped the jug and burnt myself and he berated me for my mistake. The small bathroom had one shower head inside a bathtub, one basin and a face mirror. Dad said to have a bath instead of taking me to the pools and I convinced myself that I was sick anyway because my nose was runny from crying.

We stayed in different sized rooms in the house depending on how much money Dad had that week to pay the landlord. We walked to the landlord's house on Petersham Road, with a tall metal gate, white pillars and lion statues, and paid cash. One night before bed, in one of the smaller rooms with no window, I was asked to say the prayer and kept accidentally calling God 'Miss Avangalatos', my kindergarten teacher. I was told to stand in the middle of the room while he stacked large, stone, red-painted dumbbells over my feet. I stood there in the dark until I felt wee run down my legs. In the same room, I kept the tooth I wiggled out by myself to bring it back to Mum's because the tooth fairy would visit me there. One time, another boarder called Tony hung himself on the back of his door. Days later, pink juice seeped out from underneath the crack, giving him away. Dad pissed in empty Coke bottles so he didn't have to get up and go to the toilet.

In the bigger room with a window that looked out onto Francis Street, we had enough room to set up an indoor training circuit if it was raining and I could practice defending myself with a stick when Dad went to the RSL. Sometimes when he thought I was asleep, I secretly opened my eyes and watched *Sex/Life* on the tiny television. My voice croaked with guilt when he asked me if I ate any chocolate at school that day because I did and I didn't know how to lie. In the same room, he threatened to hit me if I kept making mistakes while I was learning how to read and told me he would burn my homework — drawings of fruit — because my mum's homosexual best friend helped me. He said all gays must burn in hell and drew his profound detailed drawings using a four-colour retractable ballpoint pen. Blue, black, green and red lines showed my mum burning in hell with snakes and fire torturing her while Dad and I ascended into the clouds into heaven. I disassociated while I watched *Madeline* after school: Miss Clavel wakes up in the middle of the night, panic stricken and runs through the big house singing, 'Something is not right! Something is quite wrong!' and hurries to check if the children are OK. The closing credits meant it was time for training.

One night I decided to run away. I walked down the hallway to the bathroom in the kitchen corner to brush my teeth and left through the backyard and ran down the side of the house. I pushed open the low side gate and stepped out onto the footpath. The little blue cross at the top of St Brigid's Catholic Church shone in the distance and the Telstra telephone box lit up the other side of the road. I was going to the Francis Street sister house which was built by the same people and painted the same colour, but looked less sinister because it was north-facing and had a grass patch out the front. We met a lady earlier that day who seemed like she wouldn't be at the boarding houses for long. I went to her door and she let me in. I told her I was running away from my dad and to please call my mum.

'9,5,5,8,4,4,8,0.' She reached the answering machine.

'Hi, this is Paula and Forever, please leave a message after the tone.'

The lady started to panic and mumbled something like, 'Please, Paula...' and hung up. She hid me inside of a cupboard. Moments later, Dad banged open the lady's door and I busted out of the cupboard, side-stepped and ducked under him and flew down the hallway and threw my body down the front steps without a thought, my legs coordinating themselves.

This was one of my many flight responses. I had already jumped out of a window in Sydenham to get back to my mum, ABBA singing in the background on my dad's tiny television. I also ran out of a pawn shop on the corner of Marrickville and Victoria Road and got hit by a black four-wheel drive out the front of Victoria Yeeros trying to get to her. At that exact moment, Mum was speeding down the hill in Red Betty and she glanced at me as I was running out of the Francis Street sister house and jumped straight into the back right side of the car. She drove me to McDonald's for a ninety-cent apple pie.

One day, under my Troye Sivan Banksia

Victor Guan Yi Zhou

I force a smile in Grandma's mirror cause it twinkles my tooth gems. Got them at a salon near Parra the other day, right after Mum and Dad kicked me out. Four of them. Two on the top canines. Two on each incisor. Crystal Swarovski. $150 all up. Each gem will help me manifest my dreams. And tonight is the perfect time to attract beneficial energies. A witch on TikTok said so: 'Guess what's happening tonight fellow Geminis?' she said. 'The supermoon is coming out, so get excited.' She explained that this moon was going to sit opposite to Saturn, signalling the end of a chapter in our lives. A closure but also a beginning.

'Turn around aa,' Grandma says.

In her no-bedroom Eastwood apartment, I show Grandma my business-casual inspired Nautica outfit I swiped from Salvos in Seven Hills.

'My god. Do you want to die?' She has a flapper-girl bob and armour of pearls like Anna Wintour. With both arms she rips off my clothes, chucking them on the floor with all the other laundry. Grandma grumbles about how my ribs look like the claws of a praying mantis. I tell her I apply to jobs, write resumes, complete video-interviews and answer company questions to the point where I forget to eat. She tells me to, 'Sau de laa.' Which means, 'Shut the fuck up.'

Grandma stumbles over a Jenga stack of toilet paper rolls to get to my dead grandpa's gorilla-sized wardrobe. She swings open the double doors and dives headfirst into the junk. She pulls out a black suit, and chucks it to me with a grunt that means, 'Put it on.' As she bulldozes the rest back in, I notice a wrinkled photograph in her hand.

'Can I see?'

'Tsk, hurry up aa.'

Grandma frisbees the photo back inside the wardrobe and starts slapping the suit onto me. From the glimpse I got, I knew the photo was a soy sauce stained one that Mum once stuck on the fridge. It showed Dad and little-me standing in front of Mum's garden, brandishing her home-grown corn like harvest kings.

A week ago, Mum crumpled this photo up and threw it at me as Grandma and Dad held her back. She screeched a torrent of painful words. I shot up both middle fingers and told Mum, 'Heoi sei.' Which means, 'To go die.' Then Mum screamed at me to, 'Puk gaai aa!' Which means, 'To drop dead.' Which means, 'Drop dead out on the streets.' All cause she had caught me in my room with a cob of home-grown corn lodged up my ass.

From her jean pocket, Grandma pulls out a handful of incense sticks and a lighter. Flowers of smoke bloom out of the sticks. With both hands, she moves the bundle up and down like she's giving her dead husband a slow, sensuous wristy. Sprinkles of ash lightly dust the ALDI bag underneath her.

'Help him out aa. He's still your son...' Since I got kicked out, Grandma calls upon my parents to take me back. But incense sticks only work with the dead.

I watch her face, her lips mummified like dried abalone. Her eyes scrunch up tight, trembling softly as if in pain. I sigh and look out to the pots of dying succulents on the balcony.

'They can both go kill themselves for all I care.' She slaps the back of my head. 'They said the same shit to me.'

'Hand.' She gives me the sticks. I hold them above my head.

'Please gimme this job.'

Together we jab the incense sticks into the red delicious she keeps in her makeshift altar next to the wardrobe.

'Where's your interview? I'll take you.'

I put my phone on silent and ride up the elevator of the Macquarie Street skyscraper. The foyer's pretty empty, ten times the size of Grandma's apartment, and smells of bleach. The receptionist welcomes me as her manicured nails softly tap her keyboard. Then she tells me the interviewer will be an hour late. 'Haha, no worries!' I say as I go to wait in a chair. Fucking bitch.

The suit makes me look like any one of Lucy Liu's suited Japanese ninja-henchmen in *Kill Bill*. The ones that run in headfirst on command, shrieking, just to get absolutely cut the fuck up. But I got character. I got tooth gems — heart-shaped diamantes that the Arab lady at the beauty store picked out for me.

Three of the tooth gems will manifest me money, power and bitches; the supposed bare minimums that make a man. Mantras from a long line of overbearing Chinese mothers. But the last one represents my dream to have a space of my own — I want my very own Troye Sivan courtyard garden. And in my Troye Sivan courtyard garden, I will sip my Troye Sivan mimosa underneath my very own Troye Sivan Banksia. Sip from daybreak to night. Sip until the choy sum transforms into jade. Sip until I didn't need to think at all. And I guess I need money for that.

'Hey, sorry about the wait.'

The interviewer is a short Jimmy Fallon with a gummy smile. As he walks me to his office, I make a dumb joke about Sydney traffic and laugh. He notices my tooth gems and I can see the fairy alarm sounding in his head. 'Sorry but you don't have enough consulting experience,' he says after pretending to skim my resume.

'For a sales job?'

'Yeah.'

I leave quickly.

Instead of going back to Grandma's apartment, I watch the orange sun set over the Opera House from a wooden bench in the Royal Botanical Gardens. I watch an Asian family walking together between sun-kissed sandstone and red-flowering grevilleas, the dad's hands clasped behind his back. I force a smile at the setting sun. Sea winds tickle the tears running down my cheeks — cause right now I feel fucking dumb in the black suit Grandma wanted me to wear.

Shadows set over the garden. I hear rustling through the bushes. A person hobbling in my direction. I can feel their stare, chilling as the wind. I turn my head, standing up from the bench to face them.

They pause, steeling themselves as if I had just unsheathed a katana. I take a step forward, gum nut cracking beneath my Docs. All the lamps suddenly turn on.

'Grandma?' I say, squinting at her face. I run my hands down my cheeks like a squeegee, tears sticky between my fingers.

'Nei zou me haam aa?' Grandma barks.

'I wasn't crying,' I whisper to myself.

Quick as a gust, Grandma wraps her arms around me. She pushes me around to make sure I'm alive. Softly slapping my face, prying open my eyes.

'What happened? I called and looked for you everywhere!'

'Interviewer said I didn't have experience in consulting.'

'For a sales job?'

'Yeah.'

She clicks her tongue. 'Ng gan jiu aa, zoi wan gwo dai ji gaan laa.'

'Yeah whatever, always next time.'

Grandma squeezes my cheeks. It feels like a smooch from a baby octopus. I sit back down on the bench, she sighs and does the same.

'When is the moon showing?' she asks.

'In a couple of minutes.'

She grabs another handful of incense sticks from her jean pocket, and lights them up. The smoke hovers above us into a ghostly form. Its shape reminds me of the Troye Sivan Banksia of my dreams. Gnarled, but beautiful. We watch the stars.

'You know I'm your family, right?'

We spot the supermoon before I respond. 'Wow.' It's a mountain of grey light, slightly cloudy through my waning tears.

Grandma wraps her arm around me. 'It's okay. We hurt together.'

I force a smile in Grandma's arm. Under the Troye Sivan Banksia of my dreams. Under the moonlight.

Driving Me Loca

Natalia Figueroa Barroso

Parking Spot

At five kilometres per hour,
our car grumbles over speed humps.
Its undercarriage screeches slag
and stations itself upon
my cochlea.

Click-clack Papá unbuckles himself free.
I can feel the spark in his thoughts,
pulling at me like a rip current
flowing seaward.
Chaos beneath calm waters, encapsulates my papá.

The parking lot is full.
Yet, he steers through the carpark,
searching for red lights reversing
like a shark navigates the sea
smelling for blood drops sinking.

Someone left their headlights on.
Rusty wheel suspensions over potholes
knock the wind out of me.
My window's rolled all the way down
but the air is unmoving.

Our blinker ticks a countdown.
Every segundo that drives by,
the car's interiors fold themselves in,
closer and closer.
Almost collapsing over us.

The cassette tape tangles itself.
Like an exhaust pipe I cough,
with every inhale.

Like a punctured tyre I deflate,
with every exhale.

Papá taps the steering wheel.
I attempt to open the door,
the handle snaps at my forehand.
I jolt at it back,
the windowpane shatters into sand.

The low fuel light illuminates.
Time topples over,
filling up space.
Glass shards in my frilly socks
prick at my soles.

Child locks jam me in.
The car chuffs white smoke,
seeping fumes into my mind.
Thought a haze,
like a dirty windscreen.

I'm fastened to my backrest.
My seatbelt straps me tight
in an uncomfortable embrace.
Its steaming polyester scalds
the childhood off me.

A car tailgates our rear.
Papá turns back smiling
through clenched jaw.
Saliva ejects as he screams.
I mean speaks.

Testosterone signals in the air.
Clogging the exhaust pipe.
Drowning the rev out of me.
Estacionandome on the spot.
My bladder is full, I might leak.

Rear-view mirror reflect hand gestures.
Papá's ocean blue eyes glow
like firefly squid.
Tentacles wrap around my arms,
leaving a spiralling new bruise.

A brake jerks my gut.
I stare at the skid marks from yesterday
pressed upon my skin.
They look like a double helix.
Sangre de mi medula.

Tinted windows are a dream.
Thunderstorms rumble in my bones.
Papá's cataracts cloud his vison
but I see the wipers covered in thick soil.
Mud cakes under blade, wash away.

Swerving past exit way out.
Memories muddle my throat,
b[l]eep censor,
muffle my voice.
I'm on mute hovering over the road.

I'm space debris orbiting Earth.
Let me be weightless.
Let me float.
Let me swim through nothingness.
Let me unjam my mind.

Aggressive horns gravitate me back.
A dankness sits under my thighs, it's lukewarm.
        I slide.
I sweat.
I've pissed myself.

        'Park your culo down mija.'
Another man took our parking spot.
His lowrider roars,
        'Fuck you. My dick's bigger than yours.'
Papá gets out, leaving the door open behind him.

Freedom's ajar touch too far.
A cry pushes out of me like a bebé exiting the womb.
            '¡Mamá, Mamá ... Mamá!'
But Mamá's hiding under my bed.
Stuff toys cushion her head.

She's not a passenger acá.
My eyes monitor Papá
like security cameras.
But as he opens the trunk,
he's no longer within frame.

Temperature gauge moved to hot.
On the side-view mirror,
a baseball bat flings across the asphalt.
Igniting up my nervios.
Embers rise and soar.

Dead car battery vomits acid.
Headlamps flicker dim lights.
It reminds me of fireflies dancing in the noche.
Like stars shooting in the carbon sky.
Or fluorescent bacteria on the surface of decomposing fish.

Roadtrip

Rainbow lorikeet and windscreen collide.
Green and red feathers fly,
drifting off into el cielo.
Disembodied meat; plumage and blood.
Blinding carnage.

Papá pushes the emergency lights.
The highway zooms past us.
            'Bloody pájaro!' he yells.
His ink black hair sails in the wind.
His gaze so salty it stings.

Fractured roadmaps upon windshield glass.
Sangre trinkles into shards
cracked like veins.

Sunshine bleeds through
stained red shadows.

Beak, wings, eyes, breast, talons.
Plastic bag reserved for
carsickness, for rubbish.
Now becomes our feathered
accident's resting place.

Cigarette lighter pops right out.
The Winnie Blue blazes from radiant orange to ash black.
Smoke doughnuts puff out Papá's lips
as he flicks his ciggie.
            'Los milicos rolled one cigarro onto my cell floor, but no lighter.'

Dust clings to the dashboard.
With my right index I draw a road.
A sooty fingerprint marks my fingertip.
I don't know why he tells me these things.
Maybe trauma has an end of sentence date.

All's clean, Papá buckles in.
The sea blue sky, out my window,
is profundo. In its depths
clouds plunge and wash over azul
like the brisa envelops a bird's pinion.

Saline aromas in the air.
Murmurs of waves caressing sand,
surf over my ears.
Burnt wood fires up my
gut, it rumbles.

            'Are we there yet Papá?'
Radio frequencies are disrupted,
words cut into static tongue.
A change of gear,
soon we'll be near.

Back window frames new scenery.
The land is parched,
flaked beige soil
like my dry lips.

Into the horizon the sun dips.

McDonald's drive-thru steer into awkwardness.
Greasy fingers, sugar rush, brain freeze.
Bolus stuck to the roof of my mouth.
Monosyllable replies lead to a dead end.
Detour helps conversations descend.

       'Pronto we'll get to swim.'
The words are choked by his moving tongue
and rotating jaw.
As if speaking with a mouthful
of guilt.

Speakers vibrate over the unanswered.
Mist races up into the charcoal night,
covering us in a blurred clutch.
Fog lights unable to cut through
the dense atmosphere.

Forked road, left or right?
Gregory's under moonlight,
narrow his direction.
Tunnelling his vision.
Alarms throb at Papá's temples.

U-turn back into the familiar.
Or so it seemed.
Until we end up marking dirt
with rubber.
Mucked wipers smear our sight.

Tyre stuck in the mud.
His hardened hands begin to shovel.
Scooping up earth.
Searching for firm ground.
Instead ends up with soiled fists.

Windows are shielded by frost.
My breath dances with starlight,
like a haunting spirit.
Papá takes off his jumper
and wraps his warmth around me.

Disengage ratchet pull up handbrake.
    'Mija, we'll call it a night.
    No cucos outside to dread.
    Papá's here to hold you tight.
    Pretende que is your comfy bed.'

Pitstop turns into our destination.
Morning dew frozen onto my
raised body hairs.
I pull the hoodie's cords down,
and cocoon myself in.

Day moon kissed by sunrays.
Seagulls tango over the horizonte.
    'In el glovebox there's conflé.'
Inside sit miniature packets of Nutri-Grain.
But there's no milk, we eat puffy bricks dry.

All aquatic invertebrates are protected.
No live bait.
Size and bag limits apply.
The ashtray is filled with butts.
    'Al agua pato' — to the water duck.

Crest and trough become one.
The tide is low,
two waves collide.
Orchestrating white foam,
to curl and roar.

I dip my head under.
Salt stings my eyes,
bubbles float towards the sky.
A baitless hook cuts through the water.
Bright yellow fishing line leads me to Papá.

Caught fish convulses towards death.
Its fin slaps at the breeze.
It reminds me of a kite talking in the wind.
A flag at half-mast.
Or white sheets surrendering.

Auxiliary

Car without number plates follows.
Its hubcaps glisten with the sun
like an overpriced golden tooth.
But its front bumper is dented
like a defeated boxer's nose.

Signalling right but turning left.
Mamá repeatedly looks over her blind spot,
her wrinkled lips smile but her baggy eyes frown.
I can tell she's uncomfortable,
like torn synthetic leather is to the flesh.

Foot pressed down on accelerator.
Shock climbs up my spine and
throttles my throat. Leaving me motionless, still,
like la anguila eléctrica generates
power throughout its body, to paralyse or kill.

The speedometer indicates 125 km/h.
Out of control.
Friction; wheels scuffed by the road.
Tread worn down.
Burnout followed by blowout.

Our airbag sensors were defective.
          '¿Estas bien mija?'
With her trembling hands,
Mamá lifts my chin.
There's a bump on her forehead, swelling under her skin.

Visor mirror throws back pain.
My split lip tastes like metal.

'Perdon mi amor.'
Mamá stutters, again and again.
I resee her abraded boot on the pedal.

'Your padre's driving me loca,'
she sputters, wiping blood from my boca.
Vomit travels up into my mouth
then back down into my stomach
like petrol being siphoned.

A witness calls triple zero.
The Good Samaritan's name is Ali
but he looks like Robert De Niro.
'Do you have a spare tyre?' he asks.
Mamá breaks down, knees to the ground.

Red, blue lights, siren cries.
The paramedic wears a stethoscope
but she doesn't use it.
Mamá can't afford the ambulance ride,
tells her that we're fine.

Ali opens his fat wallet.
Debt is something my madre avoids
like cats claw themselves out of bathtubs.
So, she circumnavigates the words,
'No thank you,' upon her tongue.

'To get yous home safe.'
Before Mamá can place his money back
in his calloused hand, Ali turns around, runs off.
In that moment, I spot the car without number
plates, parallel parked across the road.

Payphone in mano, help's coming.
The minute hand does not move
on Mamá's cocoa leather strap wristwatch.
Time's cemented, petrified like the victims in
Harry Potter and the Chamber of Secrets. A stony substance.

'Is Papá a mago, Mami?'
'Your padre's a maldición, not a wizard,'
she replies, unaware that her words hurt me too.
Because if Papá's what she says he is
then, so am I. I'm a curse.

NRMA tows our Camry home.
I feel like its rusted lug nuts,
exposed and stuck.
But Mamá looks like them,
worn and corroded.

Multiple keys unlock the front door.
Inside the LED lights twinkle above our fish tank
like a disco ball at a quinceañera.
Avoiding the party, under seaweeds, pebbles and seashells.
Octavio, our pigmy octopus, camouflages. I see him though.

Meat will lure him out.
But payday is not until the day after tomorrow —
torta frita crumbs will do. I tear tiny pieces, drop them in.
The fragments of fried bread sink and inflate like
little puffer fish. The oil it was browned in spills like squid ink.

'¡Vas a kill el Octavio!'
Startled by Mamá's warning voice,
my hand whiplashes the top of the aquarium water.
I'm gonna kill him... I'm a curse. It's all my fault.
Look what you made me do, Papá's voice floats inside me.

Door knocks, peering through curtains.
Shh, be invisible like a ghost. Shh, be silent like a mute.
Mamá lays under my bed. Stuff toys cushion her head.
Under floral pillows I disappear.
Clenched fists holding onto fear.

Forced entry, the door is knocked down.
Wood smashing onto glass, Octavio crawls
onto the tiled floors. His ink reddish-brown.

Papá's dirty-white Converse High Tops
tread over spilt water. He slips.
Octopus arms tangled on hair strands.
His brackish gaze meets mine.
Where's your madre? No se. Did you crash? No se.
What happened to your lip? No se. Who was that hombre? No se.
I lie, I don't lie, I repeat, no se, I don't know.

I'm a curse, Octavio's dead.
Without giving my pet a proper send off, I left.
Without saying goodbye to my madre, I left.
Without packing any of my belongings, I left.
Into Papá's car, out of Mamá's driveway, I left.

Ruben Blades tape on the radio.
Decisiones. Cada día.
Alguien pierde, alguien gana. Ave María.
I think about who won and who lost
and imagine a woman named María.

María has long black hair.
Her eyes a dark brown
like calabash mate gourds.
Her skin earth brown
like the muddied wipers.

        '¿Estas en las nubes mija? —
Am I in the clouds?' Papá asks.
I look at the cotton in the sky and they seem free.
Free to drift and swim and hover
above, far from their silhouettes below.

'If only I could be.'
My reply sounds irrational once out of my mouth.
It reminds me of dreams that silence your screams.
Like anchors that drown and find ground.
Or bees that sting to defend and die.

There is Always a Kebab Shop Somewhere
Guido Melo

After a Night Out

Over the years and after many travels, I have experienced the phenomenon of eating after a night out everywhere. After my nights out in Bangkok, I ate pad pak boong to prevent a hangover. In Paris' 11th arrondissement there were pressed sandwiches. In Buenos Aires, after red vino on Palermo, there were empanadas. After the Alterosas mountain parties in Belo Horizonte, there was Bolão's pasta. In Peru, after dancing cumbia in Barranco, there was anticucho with corn. In Adelaide, there's gyros on Rundle Mall. And in Melbourne, the kebabs. I love ending my night in a food stall. Just like I did in Rio de Janeiro all those years ago, where I lived for over sixteen years.

Competition

Simpatia é quase amor — kindness is the first stage of love. For me, it meant something like: *Be kind to others; for one day, I may need others to be kind to me.* There is no place where this old aphorism meant more than in Rio de Janeiro.

Growing up, all the TV news presenters, all the kid show entertainers and all the advertising were with White people on them. Every time I entered a supermarket, seguranças followed me around. In my primary school, my colleagues and sometimes even some teachers called me Little Negro. From an early age, I learned that people who looked like me were not welcome.

As an adult on the streets of Rio, the police thought I was a thief. The thieves thought I was competition. The Whites thought I was trouble and business owners feared my presence. Everywhere I went, I was persona non grata.

Swiftly, to survive, I learned to factor in race in all my interactions. If I walked to a pharmacy or a business establishment too fast, I could get shot by the startled security guard. Walking too slowly would be seen by the police as 'lurking'. Running was outside the boundaries for people like me. In a way, this was a kind of protection. Because many feared me, it was unlikely I would get robbed — though not impossible.

The Journey to Lapa

At the bus stop, I hoped someone else was taking the bus towards Lapa. Otherwise, the bus driver would not stop for me.

If I was lucky enough for them to stop, the bus driver would flash their headlights at the police barricade near the bridge that connected Ilha do Governador — the island suburb where I lived — to continental Rio — to where Lapa is located. The police would then stop the bus and apply their old dictatorship techniques by pointing their guns at me and frisking me inside.

It wasn't too bad. Trauma aside, it meant that the driver and the other passengers were at ease for the rest of the trip, knowing I was not going to rob the bus. All for the cost of a small charge of adrenaline and cortisone into my bloodstream. It was an okay price to pay to have a good evening. Right? After, I would light my cigarette and chill for the next forty to fifty minutes — looking out the bus window at the fast-passing city lights.

Lapa's architecture was locked in colonial times. The Portuguese-style bairro was full of colourful houses with brown clay tiled roofs. In the centre of the neighbourhood was a white Roman-inspired aqueduct. Arriving there felt like time-travelling.

Most nights were psychotic, exciting and exhausting. I was as afraid to be the victim of violence as others were afraid of me. To some, I needed to smile to show I was not dangerous. To others, I frowned to pretend I was.

The thing with acting is that if you are not careful, you may believe in your character. Lines get blurred.

After the bus, I would arrive at a food stall and eat cachorro-quente — the traditional Brazilian hot dog. I knew the act would eventually end and I could lower my guard.

Arriving at the cachorro-quente stall following a night out was an accolade. The well-lit stall was a contrast after roaming the streets of Lapa. The kitchen was a trolley with a small stove top run by a portable gas canister and glass around the hot dogs and condiments. All contained in a silver metal case with two wheels and a handle to push. This one was run by a woman named Dona Maria. She had thick short legs, a stocky torso and soft black hands. Her nails were impeccable in red polish. Her black afro hair in a bun backwards.

My father once told me about the escravos de ganho — a brutal type of slavery where enslaved Africans could work in informal urban jobs like backcarry taxis, cleaners, street vendors and labourers — as long as they paid a working day fee for their master. The Brazilian hot dog was the great-great-grandchild of those Black people who first arrived in Brazil by force. Several food stalls are still owned by wealthy Whites who 'rent' to working-class Black people like Maria.

'A benção,' I said to Maria as I arrived, cigarette in hand and too drunk to make further conversations.

'Deus te Abençoe, meu filho — the usual?' She smiled, raising her eyebrows. She had a familiar look on her round face; judging me for my intoxicated state and worried for my wellbeing. I had seen the same look on my aunties', cousins' and grandmother's faces.

Ubuntu was an African and Afro-Brazilian philosophy of life. We saw ourselves as part of a bigger collective. I did something not only for me but for the group. What I did and what she did was part of a bigger universal scheme. My hands were her hands because of Ubuntu.

Dona Maria cooked the sausages in a stew of tomato, onion, capsicum, coriander and heaps of garlic. Then added the sauce and the sausage to a bun. It was served with mayo, ketchup, mustard, peas, corn, onion, sliced carrots, batata palha, sultanas and quail eggs on top. The slow-cooked sausage made me at ease. *All is going to be well and I will be home soon.* As Maria continued to prepare it for me, her movements were in slow motion. Her soft black hands carefully placed every condiment in its place. Feeding someone is the politest thing another human being can do — especially at 3:00am.

'Can I have more mayonnaise, Maria?'

'My son, you are going to drive me broke,' she replied with a frown and a hum sound.

The Old-School Kebab

In Melbourne, my life is no longer at constant risk. But the tradition of eating after a night out remains.

'Salaam, salaam!' I say to Mustapha, entering the neon-lighted once-white floored kebab joint in a laneway in Prahran.

For over fifteen years, the shop has had the same white plastic chairs and teetering tables covered in cigarette burn marks, anxious scratches from strangers' keys and scars with black grime inside. Vintage Coca-Cola logos are scattered around the walls. Next to Prahran's vegan and queer-friendly establishments and the many new construction sites, the old-school kebab restaurant is an ancient relic.

The smell of garlic sauce, burning charcoal and spices seasoning the vertically rotating lamb opens my appetite. The kebab is the way of my new adopted town. My new cachorro-quente.

'Salaam!' Mustapha replies, grinning behind his now greying beard.

I got to know Mustapha by applying my 'simpatia é quase amor' philosophy. I learned he was a Lebanese Muslim. I told him about the Brazilian Lebanese community in my old home. He told me that the neighbourhood used to be an area full of working-class Greeks, Italians and other Europeans. Historically, those kinds of Whites were seen as second-class labourers. Now, the area was full of Anglos, Chinese, South Asians and South Americans — all cosmopolitan and upper-middle-class.

These days, I don't have the energy for a night out that ends at 3:00am any longer. Still, I know that there is always a kebab shop somewhere, or a hot dog stall, and I am lucky to know my nights will end on a boring and comfortable bed.

Discarded Stalks
Meyrnah Khodr

Mulakhiyeh

When I'm seven, the owner of our rental sends a painter to our house in Mount Lewis. He says his name is Boo and spends most of the time pulling funny faces, which cracks his dry skin. Boo is trying to make my two sisters and I laugh. He pulls off the tip of his index finger and my eldest sister Ayah giggles — her tight black curls wobbling around a face that's as brown as the Arz tree plaque hanging behind her. She tells me Boo is just playing a trick. By the third day Mama is annoyed by all the questions Boo has about the things in our house and where we come from.

'Shi bi dayik el khelak,' she complains to Baba, her patterned house scarf slipping from its knot, 'Why must he take so much time? I don't want to answer any more.'

'Ya Salwa, ya Soos, ya habibatil kabira,' Baba reassures her, taking off his welder's cap. Mama had sewed the cap using scrap cotton. Baba continues, 'Don't worry my love. Allah will see your patience. Boo will be gone soon.'

'You should see his hair, it's as white as laban. And I don't think he's very smart, laughing with the girls all the time. Tool aal faadi,' Mama laughs, the gap in her teeth peeking out of her broad smile. We spend the rest of the night teasing Boo and his strangeness.

The next day, Mama gets up early, as she has been since Boo arrived, to make kibbi and lahim bi ajine. She says it is ayb not to feed our guests. 'No touch, no touch!' Mama waves her hands at Boo when he tries picking up a bunch of the mulakhiyeh leaves with dirt-encrusted fingernails. The mulakhiyeh leaves are scattered all over our dining table and Mama does not want him to mess up her hard work.

Before Boo came, I watched as Mama had sat with her back hunched forward and pulled each individual leaf from its stem, which stained the tips of her fingers a dirty green. Her short fingers were nimble as she worked. Sometimes Mama leaned her back on the leather couch. Other times she stretched her legs out on our colourful woollen rug. When she spotted me, Mama told me how she used to help her mother back in Lebanon prepare mulakhiyeh for her own family of ten. The leaves were slowly simmered in pomegranate molasses then combined with chicken and lemon juice to create a thick soup. Tayta taught my mama that the meal could be stretched out further when eaten with rice and warm khobz. Eventually, me and my sisters played sword fights with the discarded stalks.

The sharp smell of paint still fills the house when two policemen knock on our door. They think the mulakhiyeh drying on the dining table is weed.

My sister and I cower under the dining table where Mama had spent all morning cooking for the painter. Do the police know that Mama needs the mulakhiyeh to make our coins last?

With shallow breaths, Mama explains that the leaves will be cooked in a chicken broth. My sister and I hear the policemen's boots stomping as they conduct a thorough search. Their big boots shuffle as they touch and sniff the crinkly leaves for at least five minutes. When my sister and I look from under the table, the short officer with a pot belly packs some mulakhiyeh into a small plastic bag. Meanwhile, the other officer, who looks as if he's never smiled in his lifetime, pokes his smooth face around our display cabinet, bending to pick up the cedar carvings and antique coffee pots Mama brought with her from Lebanon.

When Baba arrives home, having been called upon by Mama, he tries to make the officers laugh but they just nod their heads as he talks.

'It's okay maate,' Baba says, imitating them, even though we always tell him it's ayb to make fun of people's accents. 'Next time you come and taste the mulakhiyeh, I call you, maate.' Baba sits the officers down as he entertains them with stories of work. Still breathing shallowly, Mama offers them coffee and the last of our Arnott's biscuits.

Taxes

My father welded his way from Port Hedland to Queensland, Port Kembla to the city of Sydney, Sydney to Bankstown. Each time, he brought home yellow pay packets filled with notes and coins that always wound up in the hands of those who asked, leaving not much left for us.

When my father arrived home, after weeks away, flecks of metal clung to his long beard while red dust from some faraway outback clung to his jeans. He told us stories about how it was so hot that he'd hang out his washed jeans to dry overnight and they would end up as stiff as his sore muscles.

The year I turned fifteen, Baba left a part of himself at the top of Governor Phillip Tower in the city. Since then, I've had to accompany him to every Centrelink visit.

'I build Australia! I pay tax and you don't help me!' Baba yells at the blonde lady behind the counter at Bankstown Centrelink. He bunches up his pant leg, rapping hard on his new prosthetic. The wooden sound echoes through the crowded office. Blondie's blue eyes widen for a moment as she fluffs up her frizzy perm. 'Sir, please.'

'Ana emarat hal balad, tfeh alaykun.' Baba shifts closer to the counter, wobbling precariously on his new limb. He tries to keep his balance. The toes on his good foot, which are showing between the woven parts of his sandals, curl inwards like roots clinging to earth. But then Baba stumbles and clings to the counter, squeezing his eyes shut as he tries not to fall. I try to steady him.

'I'm sorry sir, there's nothing I can do to help you,' the lady says with a sympathetic-looking smile.

If my father hadn't held on for so long, he would have lost his life as well as his leg. He told us how he had clung to the edge of the elevator shaft, fifteen storeys up in the air, while the only thing keeping him from falling was the thick material covering his mangled leg caught on a piece of metal. My brave baba thought of his four girls and recited Qur'an to help him stay conscious. Now Mama will have to try harder to make our coins last and Baba will love her more for it even though he'll never love himself. My father helped build Australia while Australia tore him down.

Driving a Mercedes but Living in a Rental

Adrian Mouhajer

'But like. We're not like those other rich Lebs in the Shire. We're humble. My dad's a doctor who drives a Toyota.' My girlfriend laughs. I arch my eyebrow. We're both Lebanese but her house is the biggest one I've ever been invited into. Her living room and kitchen alone encompass more surface area than my entire house. There's a fireplace underneath her flat screen, and their kitchen countertops are always pristine, accompanied by the ever-lingering faint smell of Dettol cleaner, and made of one hundred percent genuine real marble. Her parents even have an infinity pool in their expansive backyard.

Not the Mouhajer family though, we just have the peeling fake marble countertops back home. When I was younger, we lived in a house with a pool on Lakemba Street. My dad and brother kept it clean, carefully checking the chlorine levels with their pH strips every few weeks. I thought it was ours and that we were rich. Then the landlord decided to sell. My parents were pensioners so it wasn't like they could afford to put in an offer. We moved out within the next month; straight into public housing and we never had another place with a pool.

We always had a nice car though. My dad was smart when it came to cars. He wasn't a mechanic by trade, but he could figure out most mechanical problems just through guesswork. I guess that was his 'Leb ingenuity'. He had a habit of going to auction houses, and if he spied a luxury car that was basically a step away from being a write off, he'd swoop in and buy it on the cheap so that he could fix it up for nothing back home. His dream car had always been a Mercedes 4WD. When he got his first one at an auction, he screwed on a custom hood ornament in the shape of a horse, which he brought over from Lebanon when he was twenty years old.

Dad put in posh stuff for us as kids too. We were the first family in Lakemba I knew who had portable DVD screens on the backside of the front seats of our hodgepodge Mercedes. This was way before tablets and laptops were a thing so we were iPad kids before they even invented the term.

On the weekends, Dad always found ways to take his luxury vehicle out for a spin. We would go for family drives to the Leb side of Bondi and meet up with our cousins, and my dad would boast about how smooth his ride was. My mum was a big fan of the Mercedes too — to this day she says, 'I won't be a passenger in anything less than a BMW.' All this was my dad's way of making us feel rich. The Mercedes was ours outright, so I never had to worry about it being sold from underneath me.

'Y'know I'm from The Area, right?' I say it slowly to be tactful, but my girlfriend still blushes at my admission. Her thick brows furrow. She came over mine for iftaar last week, so she's seen my fibro walls.

Over the several months of us dating, my BMW had been parked in her sprawling paved driveway moreso than the patchy front yard of my parents' houso.

'Oh god,' she says and squeezes my thigh apologetically. 'Sometimes I forget that what "rich" looks like really does depend which side of the bridge you're on.'

It's my turn to laugh and I squeeze her hand back as I pop down the roof of my BMW. 'It's okay,' I say over the breeze. 'I still love you.'

There are no Beaches in Bankstown

Rayann Bekdache

The jute rug scratched Malala's crossed ankles — its faded pink hue adding a touch of colour to her Dutton Street granny flat. A small wooden lamp, a housewarming gift from her sister, lit the living room. Malala preferred its glow to the blazing fluorescent tubes that lingered in her retina and amplified her electricity bill. Bubble gum argileh wafted through the flyscreen of her solitude. Afrobeats, hip hop and pop all playing through The Area, blended like a collaboration between Stomzy, Burna Boy and Ed Sheeran. The music kept her company on this sweaty Friday night. *There are no beaches in Bankstown*, she thought, staring out at the Colorbond fence separating her flat and the Chinese landlord's house.

Another humid night; cockroaches and mosquitoes buzzing. The open flyscreen was Malala's only relief. The broken AC unit was as useless as the repair request she sent to Assured Rent Real Estate. *They won't do shit*, Malala thought and leant against the frayed couch she bought when she was still married, inhaling the sweet smoke of herbal tobacco. Sweat dripped onto the baby pink sports bra and torn undies that she wore when smoking. Aeroplanes and Wog parties echoed in the night. Each turning point in her life replayed in her head for the five hundredth time — the end of her marriage, divorce and moving out alone.

Three months ago, Malala's divorce was finalised by the sheikh at the United Muslims of Australia Centre. The sheikh's office was small, inane and sparsely furnished — its emptiness exacerbated her sadness. He accidentally reached for the marriage papers then remarked awkwardly: 'I get through divorce papers a lot more quickly these days.' Malala had been out of work for about six months before her ex-husband, Muhsin, had asked to go their separate ways. When she spoke to her Mama and Baba about living alone, they were dead set against the idea.

'Al mara mabtiskon lawahda,' Baba kept telling her, 'Muslim women don't live alone.' But after all his protests; when Malala came to her baba's tool shop asking him to loan her the bond money, he immediately gave it to her with tears in his eyes.

Two months into her iddah period — a cycle of three lunar months that Muslim women observe when their husband requests a divorce — Malala secured a job at St George Hospital in Kogarah. She was now a switchboard operator, connecting callers to the hospital's many departments. The income would barely cover the cost of the rent. Then there were her medical bills for her endometriosis and adenomyosis. She always dreaded the crimson wave and when she found out about her chronic pain conditions, it gave her a sense of relief to know what was happening with her body. Though it came at a cost of specialist fees, ultrasounds and hospital visits. All that before she could even think about utility bills and groceries.

Malala grieved. Just like her name. She had heard stories about divorced women driven into poverty. Now, here she was. But even when she was falling behind on the bills, Malala was grateful to have her own space. She preferred living pay to pay in the comfort of four walls she could call her own, even if it meant skipping lunch and dinner. Some days, Malala would drive on an empty tank and pray to Allah that her car didn't break down between Bankstown and Kogarah.

On any free weekend, when petrol would allow, Malala would drive to Little Bay. The beach reminded her of her youth and her close friend Mirna, who introduced her to the spot. They had been friends since high school and Mirna had been there in every milestone. Mirna helped Malala move her stuff out from her ex-husband's place when the divorce was finalised. Malala loved the small but attainable feeling of beauty that she could escape to when she could no longer find hope or beauty in her life.

On a particularly hot Saturday, Malala packed an apple, nuts, Kettle Chilli Chips and a large bottle of water in a cooler bag. Then she put sunscreen, a snorkel, a library copy of Elif Shafak's *Three Daughters of Eve*, a rusty pink towel, plastic beach mat and Kmart swimsuit in a backpack. Jumping in her old and beat up Toyota Yaris, Malala pumped an Afrobeats playlist down the M5 Motorway to Little Bay. She closed the windows in the tunnel to avoid the rotten egg smell. As soon as she zoomed onto the La Perouse exit, she smiled to herself, knowing she'll be by the water soon.

At the first glimpse of sand and turquoise, the tightness in her chest begun to ease. Grey chunks of asbestos, bits of rubbish and broken glass littered the sand. Putrid stormwater ran off into the sea. But she loved it, her little slice of pleasure. She unpacked her things and rubbed her body with sunscreen. After a moment, she kicked up her feet and rushed to the shore. The water gave her skin a cold shock as she plunged headfirst into the depths and swam slowly to the rocks. She breathed in and out, floating, as calm washed over her.

How to Buy a Car

Daniel Nour

I was nine when Dad first gave me the advice that would be a golden thread. A parable of wisdom — conveying in a few words all his hard-earned knowledge. He had just finished a long week at the shop we owned in the city. We were at our local shopping centre buying our groceries. He was in a woollen vest over polyester trousers and shiny brown loafers. The year was 1999 and Naughty Dog, the company behind the game, *Crash Bandicoot*, had just released *Crash Team Racing*. It was a timed go-kart contest based in the world of the mischievous marsupial. I desperately needed it.

At Big W, I pointed to the price tag with tubby fingers and asked, 'Dad, is this expensive?' He said, 'Nothing is expensive for us but you need to get good marks in your tests.'

Later, at the counter, Dad boldly asked a question to the blonde middle-aged saleswoman. Her name tag said 'Cheryl' and her hair was tied up in a black velvet scrunchie. 'Now tell me, my dear,' Dad began in a boisterous tone. 'Is this your best price?'

'What you mean, darl?' Cheryl asked with a smack of gum in her pink mouth. 'Price as is. This is a retail store.'

With burning cheeks, I walked outside, waiting at the entrance of Big W to let Dad work the trade.

On the way home, with my PlayStation in tow, I asked Dad, 'Why do you always do that?'

Dad shouted back, 'What do you mean why, bub? Always bargain! Never be afraid to bargain. If you don't ask, you don't get. Your game cube, marked it down. I saved us a full fifty dollars.'

Crash Team Racing on the PlayStation 1 became my childhood. I loved the way the controllers felt in my hands. I loved the sounds of the engine revving. I loved the vibration coursing through my fingers and wrists as I would crash into the CPU's go-kart. The CPU always picked the character of Crash himself or the deranged, straitjacket wearing kangaroo, Ripper Roo. I always chose Coco Bandicoot who, with her pink tank top and jaunty up-do, was pretty and lethal. Sometimes I played so long that blisters formed on my thumbs. On a yearly check-up, our family doctor, Dr Abdel, told me that I should play less and go outside more.

———

Every day of his life, Dad put his maxim of bargaining to the test. In theory, it could have sounded like some lofty invocation to courage, to tackle every challenge boldly. In practice, it was the more banal reality of him asking the guy at the ALDI counter if there were any further reductions on liquorice bullets.

This did not change when my dad aged into his late sixties. Even at that age, he still wanted to please me. In 2019, I followed him into the Leichhardt Volkswagen dealership. He was hunched with his sciatica, but twenty years after the release of the PlayStation 1, he still walked with purposeful confidence and carried himself with rugged but wearied charisma.

Inside the dealership, we loitered at the display Volkswagen Beetles in the foyer. Dad wanted me to feel satisfied with a purchase that would make me proud for a long time after I drove away. He also thought I was stupid with salespeople — liable to say and pay too much.

I gave the game away almost immediately. I spotted the 2014 Kia Cerato, which Dad discovered after extensive digging online, parked outside with all the other pre-owned vehicles.

'Wow, it looks great. Seems like the last owner kept it in good shape.'

With a tug, Dad pulled me aside. 'Mish t2olhom en el 3arbya 3agbak,' he hissed. 'Don't let them know that you like the car.'

Further inside the dealership, Dad began his shark game of predatory circling — vague curiosity lightly twitching at his eye. The rest of his face was graven in stone.

There was only one car we were really interested in and it wasn't even a Volkswagen. 'European cars too hard to maintain,' Dad announced, much to the chagrin of the salespeople. He continued to circle the gleaming air-conditioned lot. With his walking stick, Dad hit a hub cap here and struck a bonnet there. He was further declaring his presence to the dealership. In his home city of El Kantarra el Shar2, a small town on the Suez Canal, fishermen would throw their lines into the Gulf and wait for hours for fish to take the bait.

That day, Dad was also baiting his catch, deliberately provoking the sales staff — standard issue White guys in navy blue polyester suits. Who was the hungriest fish?

I followed Dad from afar, swallowing my frustration and preparing myself for a drawn-out pursuit. After about ten minutes, someone approached. His name tag said 'Luis'. Luis' eyes were black and beady, his teeth small and sharp, and he had a thin, slight frame. He was a cute and innocent sardine and Dad was about to slow roast him over burning charcoals.

'Yeah, hello there.' Dad's gruff tone was reverberating against the tiles. 'I'm here with my son and we're looking for something small and reliable today. Now, this Kia here. What do you think of it, matey?'

'Well, it doesn't matter much what I think of it,' Luis shot back. 'It matters how it feels to you, sir.' And with that, Luis opened the Cerato door and gestured for us to sit down.

Dad lumbered laboriously into the front seat. He examined the freshly detailed interior. The steering wheel, the rear-view mirror, the glove compartment. He glanced at the log book. Nothing escaped his gaze, nor his barrage of questions about the previous owners, registration dates and the thoroughness of the last service. Dad pulled the car out onto Elswick Street. I was in the passenger seat and Luis was in the back.

'Mr Nour, we can't really go past fifty in this zone,' Luis directed. Dad put his loafer down hard on the accelerator.

'Acceleration a bit slow,' Dad commented as he charged down a shopping strip; causing a small Asian lady to jump back from the pedestrian crossing and knock over her fabric wheely trolley.

We arrived back at the dealership. Luis' composure was intact and Dad's face was like a slate of old granite in the Valley of the Kings. But my tummy was anxious with the possibility that I wouldn't take this car home because he wouldn't like the price.

'Mr Nour, as you can see, this car is in great condition and I'm wondering if you would like to drive off with it today?' Luis offered as we stepped back into the dealership. Dad mumbled some protestations about the condition of the car. That's when Luis surprised me. 'Mr Nour, I won't waste your time if you don't waste mine. There are plenty of other buyers interested in this vehicle. If you don't like it, please tell me now and I'll see you out myself.'

This skinny Luis was no sardine. He was a Nile perch — made of firmer stuff than he looked. We learnt later that he was from Donnybrook, about 200 kilometres from Perth. Like Dad's hometown near Port Said, Donnybrook was the lesser town to a more famous city. My father and Luis had some things in common. Both men were hungry, both appreciated the value of a dollar and both had nothing else on today.

'Now Luiy, I didn't say that,' Dad replied smoothly, assigning the new nickname as we sat down at Luis' desk. 'It's a good car and we're interested. We just need a fair deal.' Dad started to list a series of extenuating circumstances that he thought might sway the austere salesman to our favour. They included me having a 'perfect driving record' and being able to pay in cash. I was suspended for speeding twice and the only thing in my wallet was an expired Medicare card.

Luis still looked unconvinced, his dull blue eyes like puddles and his pockmarked skin like an overdone fishcake. That's when Dad revealed his juiciest bait:

'We also have a good car for trade in,' he announced. 'Here's the key matey, you can go and have a look.' Luis, eyebrows raised, took the key and trudged outside to look at my sister's 2009 Toyota Yaris, which I'd been driving for two years.

A few minutes later, Luis returned with his manager. The manager was a pale man with a big belly, square jaw and red face. If Luis was a perch, here was a red snapper. Dad leant over to me with a warning. 'He's going to say some bullshit about what's wrong with the car.' Sure enough, Luis said that with the 'thumping noise' emitted by the gearbox, the scratches to the exterior, and the age of the vehicle, they could only offer a deduction of $2000 on the asking price.

Dad scoffed at this. 'You must be joking, mate!'

Luis' manager, Steve, was a man of quieter gravity than his yappy protégé. Steve told Dad that he could see how serious we were about making a purchase, but that with all these liabilities in mind and the state of the market following the pandemic, he could not go any lower without losing money for the dealership.

My heart dropped. The sound of an engine revving in the company car park ignited a vision. A countdown timer appeared before me. 3, 2, 1, race!

The wind rushed against my face. The road was bumpy beneath me. My thighs straddled the seat and the heat of combustion warmed my furry arse. My snout was long and ended in a small wet black nose. I reached up to whip the yellow hair out of my face, which was held up with a black scrunchie. This Kia Cerato was my go-kart and I was racing to win. I turned to my father, on the verge of tears.

'$14,500 is really the best I can do, Mr Nour,' Steve said.

'Stevey, my son will shake your hand today on $14,000,' Dad responded.

This was all too much. My head felt light and there was a catch in my throat. I needed a break. Noticing the courtesy De'Longhi espresso machine, I walked off and made a cup of coffee.

When I came back, I found Luis grinning a crooked smile and Dad chuckling softly. Something had changed between these two men.

The real arbitration, however, was between Dad and Steve. They were still going! 'I can't budge any further Mr Nour,' Steve declared wearily, his sunburnt face exhausted. 'It's $14,200 or nothing.' This was followed by a weighty silence like the stillness of the desert.

Steve looked at Dad. Luis picked his teeth. Dad, with his eyes wide in a questioning stare, turned to me. He had fixed the contest, but mine was the deciding vote. Would I accept the terms?

'Luis, can you throw anything else in to sweeten the deal?' I asked and Dad laughed.

'I can think of something,' Luis chuffed.

After a half-hour session of contract signing and payment transactions, I reached forward to shake Steve's hand. Thanks to Dad's ethnic bargaining, I drove off that day with a new car, two umbrellas that said 'Leichardt Volkswagen', and the feeling that I had just finished all my homework and won Time Trial in Perfect Mode.

Fences

Stories from the Asylum Seekers Centre

Detention Centre

Arash X

1. Fence

First thing you will see is fences long and thick. You will see when they say maximum security the place is surrounded with CCTVs, officers. Very thick and strong security doors from the main door towards the facility which is held the refugees, criminals and people who are waiting for deportation tickets. You will see no soul or smell any greenness, everywhere you can see people who are smoking mostly drugs to get high and forget about the time they have to kill in this facility. Every where you can see guards and ERT, those who are showing their tough muscles and their equipments like their hand cuffs. You will see even the 'clinic' which they provide for detainees to getting look after if they have health issues but still surrounded with guards, fences and ERT. They mostly provide drugs to keep everyone calm or out of this world. To keep them silence and less active for their rights.

2. Walls

The walls in detention was built with brown bricks which is high because against of fire and they are not burn. You could see lighters they built in those walls for detainees to be able to light their cigarettes. It's a piece of metal with the shape of square and it has one hole in it and behind that hole is an element to get hot and lighting the cigarettes. It also has a push button to active or turn on the element lighter behind that hole.

3. A Meal Taste in Kitchen

They feed us chicken mostly raw, uncooked. They use lots of spices which is make it sort of impossible to eat even the vegetables are frozen and uncooked so you should wash the chickens and recook them in microwave. When they serve you chicken, they serve it in tray. You could smell it's not cooked well also the vegetables they mixed with chicken it's not a good quality. They use frozen vegetables which it doesn't give you any taste of fresh vegetables. You will try to cut the chicken and you will see the blood in it and smell it so annoying then after you try to eat it even you are so hungry you will return the food or put it in the rubbish because you already lost your appetite.

4. Shower

Each building or unit facilitate it with two showers which is very small with one tap. It has cold and hot water but it was share it means there is other people are there who want to use it and sometimes they keep knocking the door and I don't feel safe or happy at all. Sometimes they use to shower to use drugs or even pee, it's so disgusting. I should always wake up early in the morning and wait for the cleaners after they done their job that was the only time I could take shower without smell or getting disturb a lot but I should always carry all my toiletries in and out with my self because other detainees will steal them or use them.

5. Adult Playground

It was a place for activity or outdoor activity. It was round circle shape with four marquees. In the middle the surface was covered by grasses and around the circle they built a cement walking path so you should walk around yourself and some activity officers sometimes had some rugby balls for detainees to play footy and the rest just sit around the marquees depending on the weather and have a chat about their legal issues, next court time and date etc.

6. Bed / Mattress

I was sharing the room and we had bunk beds so I slept at the top bed with small size and very old and broken sponge mattress very uncomfortable. The bed was next to the window, small windows with locks behind them so you couldn't open them properly, and I could hear always argue, fights, snore, crying and the smell of drugs so I never had a proper sleep never had any privacy. I just laid on that old mattress then always stuck between sleep and consciousness.

7. Smell of Drugs

I was trying to walk around and have some space but I could see the smoke keep coming out of the windows or detainees who sat outside or walk and use smokes, they all smoke, marijuana, ice etc which I am not familiar with them because I never use or try them but after a while I could recognise them through their smell which is very strong. It was burning my nose and gave me heavy headed also my eyes getting burn. It was so heavy and my lungs are start to getting hurt so it makes me cough and try to run from that spot smell of burning dry old grass mix with animals fertiliser and I always questioned myself how they can use or smell this disgusting drugs. What are their feelings or experience?

8. Conversation while they Fight

While I was on my bed, I could hear lots of conversation. Some detainees are arguing or talking to each other loudly about their court or next parcel is coming from outside and how much drugs can be in it. Others are having long and loud conversations, sometimes argument, sometimes yelling at the person behind the phone. Their spouse, their kids or parents to share their pain and suffering or ask for extra help or money for drugs, lawyer etc. Whole conversations were about crime, immigration, losing hope or next shipment.

I'm Talking about my Friend Sam

If I want to describe him for others, I might start with his body shape. It's so unique we call him skeleton with one cup of skin. With long, straight, brown hair. He is so skinny you can count his ribs also he is very tall and he has a kind and nice smile always on his face.

Describing his face, I always remember his big and blue eyes with long eyelashes also long funny nose like a bird's beak. He is so tidy and hygiene like an OCD person. He always take shower usually three times a day and spend all his money on perfume and toiletry. Also he loves to wear smart casual clothes, very colourful.

If I want to describe his personality, very funny, happy and motivated person, which he is doing his best to make everyone happy with his attitude and his jokes. Also you can get that positive energy through his voice, body language and his eyes. He is a nice dude.

Let me tell you about the event at Taronga Zoo we went before. Omg! He is totally a clown. I still giggling when I remember that how he is going around and make fun of everything and everyone. Damn. At first, his type of clothes he picked for that event was so funny — a set of pink short and button shirt which it has a big monkey picture on it (the monkey put his finger in its nose and says on his t-shirt 'the line is busy'). Then he wore a big yellow and red basketball shoes with two basketball keychain on his shoes.

Damn. He was so loud and happy. He just claim that he is tour guide and as soon as he saw the group of people and he try to explain that animal as his own friend or part of his family and how they are treat him after he feed them then he sold his story to the audience with too much confidence they believe it and I was on at the back just push my self to not explode from his jokes.

About Freedom

Khaled Elkady

Makes Trouble

My sun is very nice, same my life.

I like my pen I read I write.

This is my favourite thing all the life.

But if you write about freedom,

you will have more problem.

Makes trouble.

Then you search a new land,

to have a new sun.

So, I came here.

The Cup

He is broken

No worries I can change it but when it was broken

Something I lost

Its souvenir cup

He remember my history

I can't remember for any thing different

Journalist

Every day I go to my office.
I have my coffee early.
I write the news of my organisation.
I work ten hour.
I'm very active.

But today I had a bad news for my work.
The manager told me this month the end of all work.
You must be search another work.
Every one go out.

I went my home very sad, my wife told me, 'What happened?'
I can't tell her. Just told her, 'I'm very tired.'
My head maybe some big bomb, very noisy.

I talk on my phone to my good friend, Ahmed. I think this midnight.
I told him what happened.
I heard him when he told me, 'Take care of your self, don't go over the life.
You work to live but you don't live to work.'
'But the life have much troublation,
money very important to have a good life.'
He told me, 'Money not very thing, feeling good the important thing,
some time your feeling not true when you see money only.'

In the next day early, I went to see another organisation.
I have a new future, I can work again.
In the night I tell my wife why I look like sad yesterday.
I have a new chance.

My Home in Egypt

Mirror

In my house I feel my lovely dream, my peaceful idea, my peace.
The history of my birth, my relations.

My house is the same as my blood, its a piece of my body.
Inside my house I think peaceful ideas.

In my house have a beautiful incense smell.
My mother makes it every day, and my wife.

I like it and the smell of cooking every day.
My house has a special incense smell, it is contained by my mother.

Everything feels soft in my house.
The bed is natural cotton.

The water from the kola is very nice,
taste is the perfect temperature in the summer.

The air is best after praying fajr, it has a fresh air of pray talking,
is different.

This air give you strong power all the day. I smell it with my heart.

I hear the sound of cooking tools. It sounds like music.
Chok chok. The lovely family set around the circle table.

I can seeing her every day in my mirror,
I see her beautiful face, brown hair, green eyes, amazing talking.

Mirror

I smell her, she has special perfume, she is who my lonely is for.
I heard her talking for me, reading Qur'an, pray at midnight.

I can touch her clothes, its very soft, smokey.
I can feel her loves, she isn't dead.

She is life in my heart in my mind,
she isn't my wife only she is my friend.
My sister sharing my future, my dream.
She is all my beautiful history imagined.

At the higher of safranbolo mountain.
My sun go in my yellow home.

In every corner I saw her light,
her picture at every wall.

Her sound echo in every wall.
She is my light in black dark.

She is fresh air in the hard summer.
My jokey in sad day.

I can't tell her good bye,
I have her hand all the life.

She told me don't worry,

I'm here near you forever in inky black.

Kitchen

Kitchen is the favourite place for my mother.
She stay more and more time to make the beautiful meals.
Chicken, meat, fish, rice.
In the early time my mother get up,
after her pray go to the kitchen to bring the breakfast.

Kitchen the home of my cat (mish mish), its play and eating there.
My mother like talking the cat, like my mother talking.

Office

My office. Brown office.
This beautiful cure in my life, this cover and wide place.

In the right corner my library, its have my:
history books, lovely notes, amazing magazine.

The left corner have a sofa, read light,
its my rest place and imagine ideas.

In the front of my office two big trees, it gave me power when I lost my self.
My office unnormal, its dream place.

Bedroom Family

The bedroom family have a happy time for everyone.
Its comfort for any one, talking, jokey, sadness, happy, festival corner.

Its looks like flower garden,
maybe have all meal in, watch football matches, see movie films,
talking another family.

The centre of any one, visitors, member, friends.
If you need began your day you must be went the bedroom.

When you end the day, you must be stay in bedroom.

Bedroom very important in my home culture.

The Cook Up

Sangee X

I am cooking with Adam Liaw. When I entered that kitchen, sounds like my favourite song is playing in my ear. 'Pogiren', a Tamil song from the movie *36 Vayadhinile*. My kitchen at home sounds like a street food kitchen.

Adam Liaw entered the kitchen. Black, long hair. He wear hoodie and jeans.

His smile, looks like jasmine flower. That studio kitchen space like colourful saree.

My kitchen at home very small like rabbit cage.

I started my cooking — prawn thokku. The burner flame is high. Suddenly, Adam Liaw come and slow the burner. He come asking about my recipe. He makes me comfortable and I feel less stress because his voice is steady and attractive.

That kitchen smells like jasmine. My kitchen smells like a masala storage. That smell making me sometimes uncomfortable because mixing spices smells sometimes making me headache.

After finished cooking I started to plating my prawn thokku.

That kitchen looks like a museum because good organise and shiny pots.

Big fridge, modern veggie cutter, cutlery wooden and silver.

My kitchen looks like a closed wardrobe because my pot, grinder, cutlery all in one place.

After plating, we both taste my prawn thokku. He said spicy, masala smells and delicious, with a big smile through his beard because this is Malaysian cuisine. That kitchen tasted like silver spoon born. Big Maharaja Palace.

When I go to home my kitchen tastes like a bitter melon because this not my dream kitchen.

Dreams

Thouraya Lahmadi

All These Calls

From Auburn Station I walked down the Macquarie Street feeling so excited to go for my second writing class in the community centre. All the way, I was running to get in time to the class, laughing to myself, smelling the rain on the soil, seeing groups of grey pigeons flying on the sky and hearing this old lady with her black and tight dress shouting on the phone. She was in a call with her son or daughter, who seemed to be escaping class. The funny thing was she was speaking in Arabic, she was saying ███.

Arrived to the centre, I went to the classroom. It's a nice place as it's very big, very clean, with a big table on the middle and comfortable chairs. On the left side there is a long table full of snacks, some grapes, biscuits, coffee, tea and crumbly muffins. Our two teachers are here, and some of my colleagues. I was sitting down, preparing myself to start when my phone rings. Buzz buzz. That was my daughter calling. I apologise to get the call, go outside to answer.

I could hear my daughter crying and arguing with someone in the phone. 'Can you please, Mum? Come pick me up now. I had a problem with my science teacher again.' She was asking me to come pick her up because she's in trouble with one of her teachers. I was start getting anxious when she said, 'My teacher is going to talk to the deputy principal and put me in trouble.'

I replied, 'Don't worry, Aya. I'm coming now to talk to the teacher.' But I was feeling annoyed by this call that disturb all my plans about my writing class. I was shaking, thinking about all the last year when I was receiving calls from the school about my daughter's behaviour. *Oh! My God. I'm enough with all these calls. I hope just for one time a good call saying, 'Your daughter is doing well.'*

I finish the call, get quickly my bag and leave the centre to the school. The school was five minutes away from the centre but I was feeling so nervous that the way seems so long.

I arrived to the school, getting down the stairs and standing in front of the office door. I get a deep breath, then, ring the bell, zzz zzz. Then go inside and introduce myself as ███████'s mum. The lady in the office, who was in her fifties with blonde hair, brown shirt, black pants and a big smile on her face, asked me to sit down and wait from the DP to call me for a quick meeting.

Five minutes later, I was in the principal's office. It was a small office with a big desk on the middle and a leather couch in front of it. The principal was a lady also in her fifties, with brown, straight hair, blue shirt and black skirt, having black heels shower her touch of elegance. She started by introducing herself.

'I'm Miss ███████. Deputy Principal of ███████. How are you going today?'

I replied, 'I'm ███████'s mum. I'm fine thank you, it's nice to meet you...'

Field in Guildford

My son ████████ is ten years old. He's an average height and he is skinny. He has a tanned skin like me, curly brown hair which grow very quick, big dark brown eyes, a small nose and small mouth with thin lips. He is a very active boy who can't stop moving. He adores soccer. He has a nice smile that attracts people quickly to him. He is a friendly boy and behave kindly with everyone. He is someone who is confident and proud of himself. When he wakes up in the morning he has his dad's smell, which is like these kind of flowers that grow in the desert, a very strong smell.

I feel happy when I've got him in my arms and feel this warmness covering my heart. He is a noisy boy when he play with his PS4 and start be involved in game shouting, 'What are you doing?', 'Stop!', and 'I win!'. Being angry when he lose, 'Ah! No, I lost that's not fair.' But this is a quiet boy also when he prays and silent reading Qur'an.

In this huge field in Guildford, this skinny boy of ten years old, running like a panther jungling with the ball. With his curly hair flying in the air, I can hear his voice asking other players to keep going with the ball or passing the ball to him. This small and tiny piece of chocolate was so active in the field. Doesn't stop and doesn't take a break.

After a while from the start of the game, he got the ball from his friend and he throw it in the goal. His first goal was beautiful so that he start crying and running on the field imitating his favourite soccer player, Missy, in his signature when he goals; dancing and laying on the grass. There was many heads in front of me, running from one side to another, but his curly head was unique for me, because it's mine.

I was feeling so proud of my son because he was full of energy, enjoying this game, screaming of joy when he or one of his team screaming of joy when he or one of his team goal. These little heads, multi-coloured between the brown, the blond, the black, running after this small ball. Each one trying his best to get it and run to the goal to make a goal and get an applaud from all these people who come with their kids with a shared dream of becoming an international soccer player.

I was hearing other parents screaming, 'Go Ali, go, go.', 'Mitch, get the ball.', and 'Good job Umar, you're the best.'. The field was full of people and families coming with their kids and even with their babies in the prams. Everything and everyone around me shows different as you can see us, as parents, jumping, crying, applauding like a kid, laying on the ground and screaming, 'Ya Allah he did it.' You know some of them had tears on the eyes. I was there standing and waiting with impatience trying to jump the fence to give a push to my son feeling my heart beating quickly, worried that it explodes when his goal comes.

The game lasts for one hour but we felt, as parents, the time endless. Feeling attached to these small bodies who try to make their win. Passing the ball to the best player sometimes. Jungling with the ball. Making even faults because they were impatient to put the ball in the goal. They were all sweating, red faces. Some of them were clearly tired ask their coach to get a rest.

Tunisian Accent

I was walking in a narrow long street. It was early morning. My watch shows 6:00am, a surprising wake up for me, as I don't like wake up so early. I was feeling the breeze of fresh air with a warm light of sunrise in its first hit. I felt strange because everything around me was different: houses are tight and close to each other and painted in white and blue. The walls on the sides were made in cement and when I touched them they were crispy. I took a long breath smile when I heard pigeons and birds chirp flying in the sky blue, clear like a beautiful woman's face. This gave me a feeling of happiness and peace inexplicable. However, I don't know where I was.

I should confess that something from my inside told me it was not the first time in this place, everything familiar and strange at the same time.

I continued walking to attempt the end of the street, which was straight, then turn right. At the end of the street, there was a particular house that attracted me with its old door painted in blue and white with some ornaments engraved on the door made with two sides. I was trying to knock the door but it was open. I pushed it to find myself in the living room: on the sides, two old brown couches made with leather, an old grey rug on the floor, the yellow walls had scratches in somewhere and seemed to be not repainted for a long time. In the front side, a huge smart TV dominate the wall which contrast with the whole image of the living room.

On one of the couch, there was a lady in her seventies sitting and watching an old movie. Wrinkles found their way in her face since a long time ago. Small black eyes that remind me the black olive in my home country. She was scarfed with an old, brown, long scarf and still in her pajama red printed with black dots. The lady was short.

Suddenly, I noticed the movie was in Tunisian accent when the lady looked at me. Stand up with an expression of surprise on her face, calling my name. 'Thouraya. Thouraya. When did you arrive? Is this you?'

I couldn't say anything except throwing myself in her arms to smell the warm of my mum's lap, her breath and her smell, the same smell, never changed. It's her preferred soap of Nivea, she is always using in shower. I missed this smell for a long time. This time was the apogee of my happiness. My heart was flying for this meeting waited for years. My hands closed on my mum's body, being scared that she disappear. My tears and hers kiss each other and mix together. In my heart there was many words to say. In my mind, more and more in my mouth, there was just one. 'Mum, I missed you.'

Suddenly, I felt like shaking and another voice coming from nowhere saying, 'Mum, wake up, you didn't turn off the oven and the dinner is burning.' I opened my eyes so big, choked.

First House

It was my first house inspection in Australia. I went with my children for the inspection of the house located in Guildford. When we arrived, the first thing we found was the high grass yellow and dry in the front yard which gives a horrible image of the house. On the left side, there was a 'laundry' out of the house with no working tap, the owner said he is going to send someone to fix it. Then, in front of us there was some stairs, an old house built with timber, a dirty door, we went inside. The house was so small for six people. A tiny kitchen with oily walls, broken oven, the stove was so greasy. The sink was blocked. The bedrooms were so small with no built-in wardrobe except in one bedroom. The floor was timber and there were cracks in the walls.

ESHAYS

Stories from Leumeah High School

Land of the Long White Cloud

Lexus Katipa-Poa

In loving memory of my Papa Mardy Poa 01.03.16

I remembered this feeling. The ice cream melted in my hand, dripping down my arm. Smelling the corner bakery with their Big Ben mince and cheese pies. And walking into Countdown with no shoes on. Living in Papakura was the best. All my family was there. Nan, Papa, all my aunties and uncles with my tribe of cousins. We were all down the street from each other too.

Then we moved to Australia. Everything changed. I changed. I was young. Moving from a whole different country I repeated school, had to make new friends and adjust to life here. It's different. People stare at you weird if you don't wear shoes to the shops, they call jandals thongs and they have no Big Ben's pies, Countdown and Wendy's. I miss going to Rainbow's End on my birthdays. And I miss seeing my family. But I miss my nan and papa the most. Every time they call they say I sound more Australian than Māori.

It's funny but I have changed a lot. I listen to K-pop, I've tried to learn Korean. I might have lost my way, but I'll never forget where I'm from. New Zealand. The land of the long white cloud.

Tama o la'u tama

Brennae Danielson

1. They are asking me to connect to my culture. Which one? I'm half-caste after all. I know a bit about my culture, but not a lot. I want to know more but I am not great at drawing or writing and that is the main part of art, isn't it?

2. Connecting to my culture. Connect. Feso'ota'i. Wait... let me ask... I should know these words right? Ugh. The feelings of not knowing are as bad as not being great at art when I am creating an artwork.

3. What should I create on this journey? That is only mine.

samoan / australian / half-caste / plastic / me

4. A memory: it is coming on strong. A memory so vivid, the aroma, the newly taught experience of a traditional hot beverage in my early years. This memory is not a half-memory. It connects me to my culture and my grandparents. I am ten again. In their backyard, matua matutua (grandparents). Nan and Grandpa are here too. Along with Biron, Jeriah, Jaelyn, Braisyn (as well as myself). We are watching Nan. Is it the memory itself or the photo that I so vividly recall? She is telling us, teaching us, showing us how to make Koko Samoa. 'This is how you make it. O le ala lea na e faia ai.' The fire has started and the smell of smoke is both thick and comforting. She is moving quickly as she places the pan over the fire and starts to roast the cacao beans. I hate Koko Samoa but I am so excited to watch this and learn. Is this what connecting me to my culture is all about? The beans are roasting (tunu). Nan is teaching us the art of roasting the Koko Samoa with each step of the process.

Cacao beans are bought maka (raw) pre-packed. On an open fire pit (made of stones and woods), the cacao beans will then be roasted on a flat pan. As the cacao beans are roasted, the beans will turn into a dark brown, almost black colour and the shells will start to burn and peel off. Nan will then place the cooked beans into a kagoa (mortar and pestle) to be crushed, until it is of a thick, liquid consistency. It is then poured in a small plastic bag inside of a cup. Then, you let it sit until it is ready. You know it is ready once it is hard, ready for the next process (boiling into a hot beverage).

5. Another memory: my matua matutua (grandparents). Inside their house are photos everywhere. Family. My Family. La'u Aiga. They are constantly staring at us, reminding us of our importance in Nan and Grandpa's lives. They decorate the walls with cultural ornaments, with falas (women grass mats), reminding us of OUR importance to them every time we arrive. Filled on the other empty spaces of the wall. A blue ie lava lava, filled with the names of their children (fanau o matua o lo'u tama) and grandchildren in black and gold. Do the houses of my friends' grandparents look the same? Is their culture as strong as mine? Lotonuu. Is the front yard of their grandparents' houses lined with a well-kept garden, where they spend a lot of their time? Do the greens of the garden provide them with the same comfort that they do for me? Do their grandparents send them into the kitchen to check the cupboards and freezer for ice-creams and chips they earlier purchased, expecting our weekly visitations?

6. I guess even when you don't think you have a strong connection to your culture; a memory; memories can prove you wrong pretty quickly. There is nothing half about my time with my grandparents or about being their tama o la'u tama.

Them

Zo'e Laufoli

i'm their therapist.

i'm their school mother.

i'm their protector.

i'm their angel student.

they tell me their problems, but i can't tell anyone mine...

i am not your therapist!

they want my help and advice, and yet no one gives it back...

i am not your mother!

they start battles and expect me to finish them, and yet i fight my own alone everyday... i am not your protector!

they want me to be good, no matter what i'm going through, and yet everyday

makes me psycho... i am not your angel student!

to them, i'm just that... but to me,

i'm a friend... i'm a daughter... i am a person... but most of all... i am a kid.

Gutter

Stories from Macquarie Fields High School

Untitled & Anonymous

At recess I went to the oval with my friends. Five minutes before the period 2 bell, we went to the canteen. The bell goes off, we headed to class.

At recess I went to the oval with 3 of my friends, they are all Filipino, they have all been my best friends since 2017. We were walking to the canteen, we walked past the school therapy dog, her name is DJ (Daisy Jane). On the way to the canteen a year 9 student who is like a little brother to me jokingly said he would blow up my head. My friends and I arrived at the canteen, the youngest but tallest one said she was going to buy me coffee, we both lined up but since I got served first, I felt like a good friend so I offered and bought her a coffee. Then the period 2 bell went and my 3 friends dropped me off out the art block and they headed to their English class.

My 3 Friends

- clarisse : filipino, oldest, wears glasses, same height as me.
- yasmina : filipino, second oldest, same height as me and clarisse. always has a totebag.
- shabnoor : bangladeshi, third oldest, second youngest, same height as clarisse and yasmina, wears hijab.
- maureena : filipino, tallest, youngest, has a bts bag.

being able to buy a new home
AND be on top of bills
MONEY

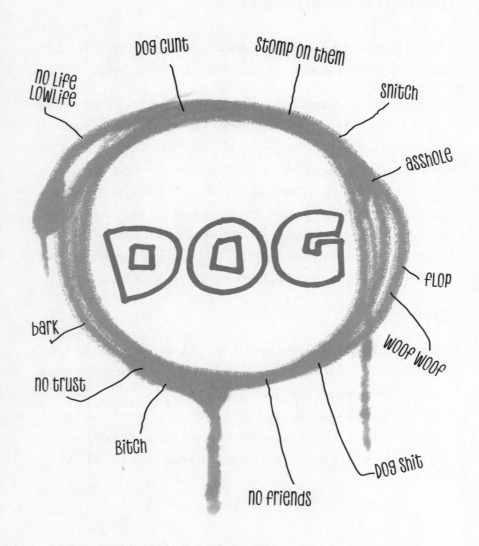

Bitches before snitches

Bros before hoes

Sisters before misters

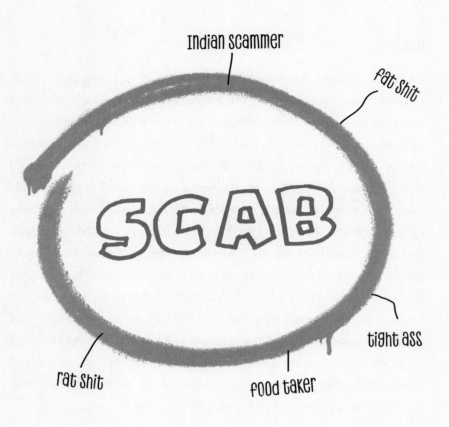

Indian scammer

fat shit

SCAB

tight ass

food taker

rat shit

A year 8 girl scabs food off all/most of the people she knows in the school

OPPS

Home

Home is a place or something that holds memories. Home to me is my uncles house in Bangladesh, in my uncles house lives my uncle, his wife, 1 of his daughters, his only son, my cousin brother wife, my second cousins 1 boy my age and 1 girl 3 years old, also my cousin sisters only daughter 9 years old, and lastly our maid who is like a grandmother to me. Although 9 people is alot in 1 small house, it is very cosy and safe. That place holds one I'll never forget. In 2012, we went to Bangladesh, we took an 8 hour long drive from Dhaka (the capital of Bd) all the way to Pabna, a small city in the Rajajshahi district, when we arrived to my uncles house in Pabna, we stepped out of the car to see all the family, waiting for us, my dad who is 1 of 8 children, spots his younger brother in the crowd waiting for us in the front yard facing the main road. He starts — crying, it was my first time seeing my dad cry, as a little 6 year old at the time I found it funny seeing such an old man cry. I asked my 11 year old sister 'why is dad crying (abbu keno kadthese)', she whispers to me 'his mum passes away when you were 2 years old', then stopped laughing, cause.

Untitled & Anonymous

things my parents hit me with

fly swatter
    BROOM STICK
  wooden ladle/spoon
      sandal
          shoes
        weird look CHAIR
metal broom stick

In year 5, 2 days before my 5&6 grade farewell, I was playing outside in the street with my neighbours, one of my neighbours son, a little white boy who was about 7 years old with Adhd and anger issues. We had a small conflict while playing but his anger towards the small conflict was huge. My red Razor scooter that I got from the Salvation Army as a Christmas present was really sharp in a few parts. I laid my scooter on the driveway. The little white boy pushed me to the ground and I fell onto the sharp parts of my scooter, my back had cuts and bruises in a straight line because of the scooter. It hurt alot and I went back home crying. I get in the house, my mum, a short fat wrinkley woman, she was mad. I cant even remember what I did wrong but this fat bitch of what I call mum starts yelling and slapping me, she whips out the metal broom stick and hits me in the back exactly where my neighbour pushed me and my back got bruised. I screamed and cried so loudly, my parents didnt know I had got hurt just before my mum whacked me with the broom. I ran to my little storage/bedroom crying. The next morning at school, I was still really upset, I went to school in alot of pain. The teachers surprisingly noticed that I couldnt sit or stand properly, two of my teachers took me out of class and I started going off, crying about my neighbour pushing me and my mum hitting me with the metal broom stick. We had a conversation but I was so traumatised that I cant remember what was being said. The next day was my year 5&6 farewell. This short Asian man came knocking at our house. My dad was talking to him, I went into the living room and my tall, scary, big eyed glasses dad told me to sit down and talked to the Asian man.

I remember the man introducing him self something on the lines of 'Hello my names Van and um from Docs', man I have a Dory brain, cant remember fuck. Later after talking he said that I have 2day to think about if I want to go to a Docs house. At that time I really wanted to, Id get to experience living in a new different family and I can get away from my shitty family. The man left my house and I quickly got ready and headed to the formal. 2 days go past and the man comes back to get an answer if I want to go or not, I decided to not go cause Ill miss my dad, he said okay thats fine but if you have an problem just call me. Van and my dad was talking about my studies and I remember hearing my dad say my math is bad, a week later Van came to tutor me, this went on for a few months.

It was the end of year 6 and I had my last tutor lesson with Van. He gave me a gift it was a little cat toy in a basket. Van helped me alot with my math and my family problems, but after he left all that shit with my family started again . . .

fuck

Untitled & Anonymous

in our area

Lebo boys are rich cunts, wearing Loui bum bags, wearing shoes that havent even been released yet, full wearing trackies and Loui glasses the bloody rich cunts wearing gold chains and gold watches n dat.

Fobs

Eat a lot
Fat cunts
Fat wide nose
People are mostly scared of Fobs
Loud / noisy
Always start fights / Trouble
Scab other people's food

I got called a 'Fob' from a white bitch at woolworths because I bought the last piece of Butter or Box.

I got low on my business exam and my teacher called me a Joke expecting me to get High marks the fucken white cunt pussio.

My uncle in Samoa was eating bubble gum at night and the aitu slapped his Jaw and his Jaw was permanently crooked.

My mum was playing with rocks at my country at night when she chucked a rock somewhere in the distance in the dark, as she went to go turn on her ride, someone threw it back at her and she got scared.

So my mate was laughing at my other mates Joke and a random Junkie said what are you laughing at and told all of us to come over and then he was holding a cracked glass bottle and then he started spitting at us and his train came and he left and starting screaming at us while going in his train and we were minding our own business.

GSO

I remember I had a fight with Elijah in primary school, it was about touch, I cant fully remember but I think he was cheating and I got angry and me and my Fob knife/wife crushed him on the gate and then we jumped him, and we got in trouble and suspended.

Tomah From Tongo

I remember one I told my mum I was going to the shops with my girl mate and we did, so we went and we left at 10:00 in the morning and we both came back at 6:00 in the afternoon and she gave me a mark on my neck, and my mum seen it and she told my sister about it, that my sister gave me a hiting with her own bare hands and slapped me around like a little bitch.

I remember I took a Lebo cunts Shisha pipe and I ran away with and then 60 Lebos were trying to look for me in Bankstown station and I was hiding in the Bankstown elevator in the train elevator.

chest x tricep
bicep x back
shoulders x traps
leg day
abs day

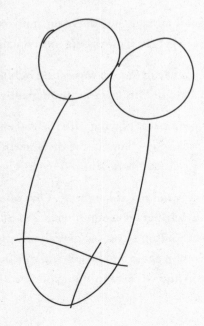

Untitled & Anonymous

Lebos

Rich cunts
New shoes
New haircuts everyday
Having a fat nose
Nice food
Fresh trackies

Fobs

Fat cunts
Eat everything
Never bring der own lunch to sch
Always eat other people lunch

White Shit

I went in to a shops to buy a drink but I could see the owner looking at the camera n keeping a good eye on me.

One day I was with one of the white boys in a car n we were dropping a bag (the white shit) to the city n the guy that was buying the bag jump in the car n he gave the money to me n I counted it n it was short so we jump him in the car n kicked him out.

Untitled & Anonymous

Woke up and went hospital with mum and saw a guy in a wheelchair with only one leg felt sorry for the bloke and then went to see Tim Spicer my doctor and he was a bold dog.

Violence

had a footy had a fight and then it went on after the game in the parking lot.

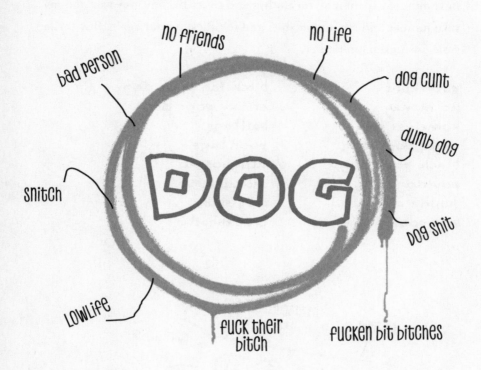

I ain't a snitch. Bro's before Hoe's. Just finding that I am going back to fiji and getting to see my family and grandparents and running with my couins at my grandparents farm and helping out grandpa with the farm and my grandma giving me and my family love try to get our favourite food even tho they don't have much money but I'm thankful for what I got — my grandparents house was white single storey house and my grandpa's toyota car and my grandpa's hut smelt like old people and have heaps of sugar cane.

1. When I was working my first job and I got payed and felt rich the next minute I spent it all on clothes and felt fucken poor again.

2. When I was working my first job and I got paid $350 and felt rich the next minute I spent it all on clothes and shoes like my grey asic and my nike jumper and champion shirt and felt fucken poor again. Btw taylla stole my fucken jumper.

poor cunt
no money
homeless dog
white poor dog
black poor dog
pov dog
junkie dog
hoe poor dog

bitch fag poor dog
cricky poor dog
ballbags
poor bags
druggos do
shitcunt
dog shit
crackhead

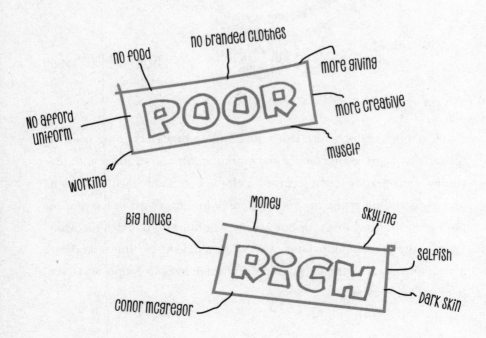

Untitled & Anonymous

Lebo

Fucken rich cunts
They got connection
They own a lot of business
They can pretty much fucken get anything:
like fucken unreleased clothing's and jewellery
They always think that their right in fucken arguments
They sound like their fucken taking a shit when they talk

Fob

Love our fucken food like fucken KFC, always think were hard cunts, I reckon we are, not gonna lie, were always involved in a scuffle, and were always used in stereotypes at school, we like to make jokes about each others dad but we never talk about each others MuM.

What you looking at

I was smiling at my mate at the other side of the station cause I was asking him for money, but I saw the guy looking at me and as I turn around and he walked forward and he said what do you have an eye problem lad so I laughed at him and I was like WTF lad. So he said do you wanna have go lad and I was like ye slut so I walked over with fale and lijah and he ran down to grab a broken glass bottle.

Micro-aggression

I get called a coconut and was told to go back to where I came from, or whenever I do one little mistake, they'll be like must be fobs or must be islanders. Got accused for doing something in the toilet and she kept pressuring me to tell her what I was doing in the toilet. The pigs pulled me over on the street cause I looked like someone that their looking for. Theres a story about a girl running around in a white dress with blood on it, in Macfields station and apparently people hear her screams at night. My old man stayed home by himself and he experienced some scary shit bruh he told us that he heard some weird noise in the house so he called my name but he realised he was at home by himself so he went to check out and when he came back he heard the piano in my room playing.

Fight

I was involve in a fight in primary school with a Leb student. It was over a footy game he was one of those Lebs that act like a fucken hk (hard cunt) so I offered him out when he was going off because of the footy game at lunch, so we started throwing hands at each other and ended the fight with an uppercut and his nose bursting with blood. On photo day yuin pushed me over because I was getting fruits out of the fruit bowl and he thought was one for Aboriginals so I held him by the shirt.

My whole crew different.

Pull up to the scene, all them pussy's disappearing.

Banging on net thats all IM hearing.

Cant step to me and my team, we want the same, so pussy stay in your lane, ill smoke you like Mary Jane.

My boy's cant be tamed, their heart is in the game, big or not, ill run him down.

Untitled & Anonymous

Violence

Growing up around violence has taught me that it is the only answer. Seeing my cousins my older brothers fight every weekend because they were protecting our mums from our dads.

- vaccum
- wooden spoon
- bbq squere
- bed
- lamp

'why are you crying'

A typical islander family suppresses their kids emotions and ignores family problems. Uncles you can't trust aunties that tear you down because of how you act and look. You can't speak out because you don't wanna break bonds and ruin everyones peace.

Independence is something that I want to do. Even though living under the same roof as my parents I would like to be my own person instead of being what my family wants me to be.

Its tempting to be what they want me to be but IM my own person. Why would I destroy my peace and be what everyone wants me to be?

My parents bribed me to go to uni and they will buy me any car I want.

Fobs

- corn beef
- bankers
- jobless
- high school dropouts
- fat
- under developed
- un relevant to society

Death of friends
scream in my ears.

The several chapters
of life.

Untitled & Anonymous

Home

Home to me is my mum. Even though its not a place she makes me feel secure, warm and loved as a home would. She has sacrificed everything and will still do it to this day. From clothing to food. My mum played both roles in my life a mum and a dad. No matter where we lived to tight fitting apartments, to big houses living with family members my mum was still my home.

We struggled to live but my mum still managed to put a big smile on her face and act. I thank my mum for making me feel secure.

I don't trust many because of my past experiences with friends, family and acquaintances.

Rules of how not to be a dog !

- dont trust that are friends with your opps
- don't nitch
- keep your circle small

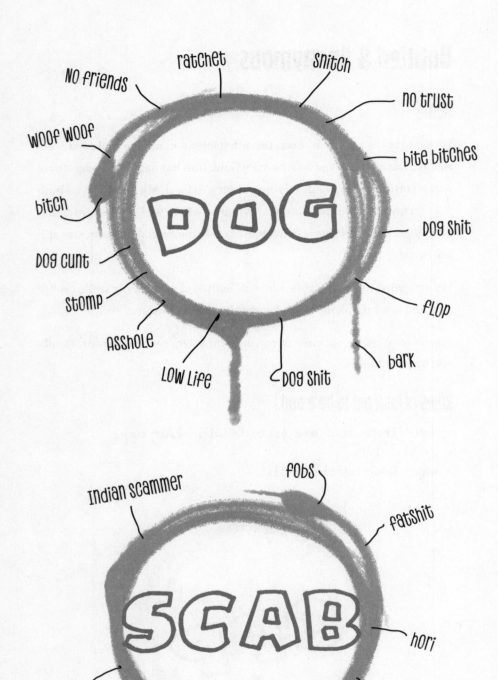

ratchet

No friends

Snitch

no trust

woof woof

bite bitches

bitch

DOG Shit

DOG cunt

Stomp

FLOP

Asshole

bark

Low Life

DOG Shit

Indian scammer

fObs

fatshit

hori

tide arse

Ratchet

Untitled & Anonymous

Take 1

I walked to Mac fields to shops. And on the way there I went to cross the road and almost got hit by a car. And from the shops I bought food and went home.

Take 2

I walked to the shops after school, I wasn't bothered to cook so I was on my way. I was crossing the road when a toyota car almost hit me. An Indian guy was sitting in the car when I swore you fucken idiot watch where your fucken going. So then I walked to the kebab shop, bought a snack pack, I ate there. Then walked home safely.

Take 3

After a boring depressing day at school I came home hungry. A hour later I got too hungry. I had cash on me so I was going to walk, walk up to Mac fields kebab shops. So I was on my way. As I was crossing the road an Indian in a toyota corolla almost hit me. My heart stopped. I swore at the guy saying 'you fucken idiot watch where your fucken going'. The Indian guy put his hand out saying sorry. I continued to walk to the kebab shop. I bought a medium size snack pack. Just thinking it wouldnt be my last. I ate at the kebab shop finishing my food. So I walked home safely acting like Im still hungry so I don look suspisious.

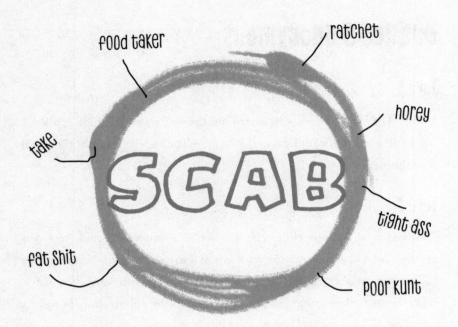

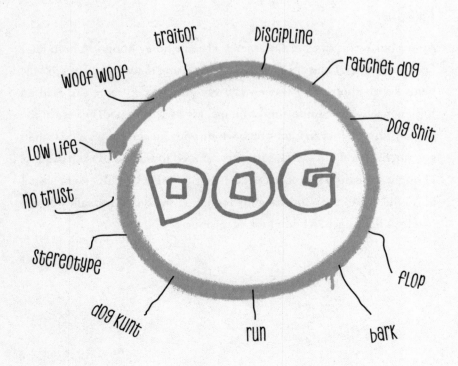

Home to me is my kitchen. Right when you walk through the door you look to the left and see yellow cabinets. My cabinets shaped like a c going sideways, with a big window in front of the sink, I have a six seater dining table only seating half the family at a time. The stove is my part of the kitchen cause im a chef when im bothered. I have a white fridge with plumbing/electricity stickers. I feel like this is home because it brings my family together.

broom shoes slippers belt stop crying

I get angry when my little siblings dont listen to my parent when told to do things. So I step in and hit them to listen to them.

dumb cunt, fucken idiot, useless to society, flop, crackhead, junkie, stupid cunt, ratchet, scab, horey, stinkey cunt

CUNT, KUNT

Untitled & Anonymous

I felt rich when playing when playing games on ps4 and I had lots of money.

I felt rich when when I get paid, and I get to buy stuff I want.

I felt poor when seeing that the selective kids have brand new iphone 12s, the newest mac book, the latest model of airpods, when I used to have an iphone 6plus and no other expensive items, when I see them walking around with nike clothes and shoes, it brings me down because I dont have branded clothes like them.

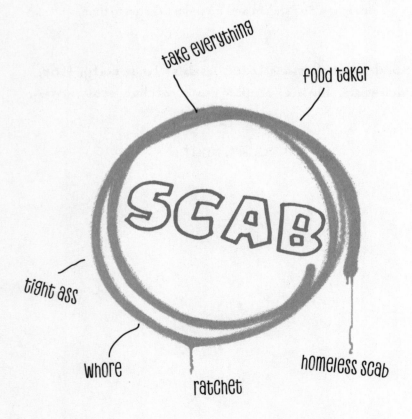

blonde ~~blonge~~ blonde
girls

lip fillers

eyelash extensions

lots of shoes

money

- satisfed

flexing

lambo

skyline — rich

- Big house

Jewellery

selfish

expensive
clothes

buy useless stuff

Working alot

No holidays

Not much food

homeless

Poor — No branded
clothes

No school
uniform

more giving

more creative

- I felt poor when comparing
myself to my peers when
they had more expensive
things to me

- I ~~g~~ felt poor when
my friends get paid
more then me.

poor cunt

no money cunt

fucken poor dog cunt

homeless cunt

povo cunt

poor dumb cunt

drugo cunt

junkie cunt

rachet cunt

piss poor cunt

scab cunt

no ciggies cunt

i'll roll you poor cunt's

stinky cunt

have a shower cunt

dog shit

"GOT A CIGGIE CUNT"

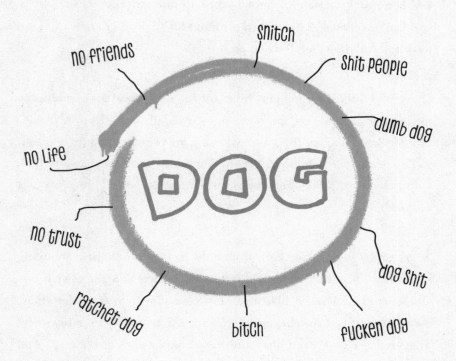

no friends

snitch

shit people

dumb dog

no life

DOG

no trust

dog shit

ratchet dog

bitch

fucken dog

I was getting scabbed when my group of friends kept using my vape when I said no, so it made me very annoyed because it would only last one day but I aint No Snitch.

I miss my grandpa alan because he was the only one that listened and I remember he always used to give me vanilla ice cream in a cone when my mum wasn't, his in heaven but his always around. He was my home because he made me feel safe and loved, he use'ta always pick me up to give me a kiss, and a big hug.

Untitled & Anonymous

1. When I got home from school, I asked my older brother for my JBL speaker, he refused and punched me and said 'fuvk off'. I knew I was too weak and then I left the lounge.

2. 3:15 pm I walked through my front door and there was music pumping in the lounge, mats on the floor, the sheets all messed up. My older brother Saulo had my JBL bombox, angry me I shouted to him to pass it ya flop. He refused and then punched me straight on the arm and then with a deep voice said 'fuck off'. I knew my punches are too weak so I walked it off.

3. 3:15 pm I walked through my front door and there was music bumping in the front lounge. 'Retaliation is a must' I knew straight away it was Onefour The Message blasting. Mats and chair sheets everywhere, older brother big Saulo the gronk stole my JBL boombox from my room. Triggered as I am I asked him 'why do you have my speaker kient?'. And tried to grab it. He straight hooked me in the mouth and said in a deep voice 'jaq kient I lost mine at work let me use yours'. I knew my hits won't hurt the gronk so I walked it off.

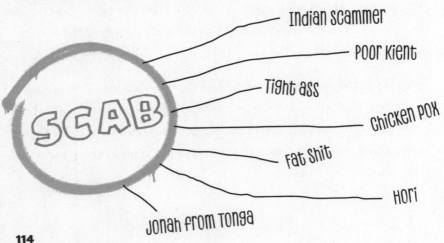

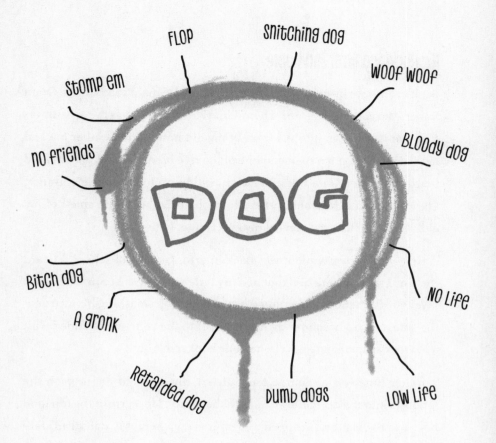

'A favour'

Dog: I Ain't A Snitch, when it's me being dogged or someone that's close to me.

Scab: Due time was when I was at school, I pulled out my chicken sandwiches and some random dogs tried to scab. So I stomped the gronks (dog).

Rules to not my dog

- don't be a snitch
- only chat to the boys
- don't be a lil bitch

NZ, Auckland Otra: 2nd Home

Back in 2010 we lived in Otra, I remember all the main roads to the Otara Super Market and to from where I stayed. The big massive Christmas tree that was grown into the front of my old house, I remember me and my sister would put a swing on one of the tree branches and play. My old house was sitted on a hill and stairs leeding up to my house entrance. Plants and fruit trees along the side of the drive way. The smell of my childhood all from the view of my 2nd Home, I miss it all.

A time when I was violent was back in yr10, last day of school. I heard the word that a gronk had touched my little sister near her private areas. I waited after school and jumped him. I ended up smashing his face onto the gate, and body slamming the gronk onto the concrete. It ended with a 10 week suspension and a behaviour book to fill out.

Another time was at church tona'i (feed), my dad told me to pach the leftovers into the car while he talks to the pastor. I lost grip of the top food box, and the last box dropped and spilt everywhere. My dad dead stare right into my eyes, and landed two massive slaps to my face and gave me a long ass lecture on the way home in the car.

List of weapons: parents used

beer bottle
water hose
chain
belt
wooden spoon
chain

FUNNY LINE: It's sad but it's the truth but most inmates got bum fucked in jail.

'The pastors house'

'Oi dickhead get in the car addays said we have to go to the pastors house,' my older brother shouted. Music pumping, windows down, we pulled up to the house and met with our cousins in their garage.

'Fuck Lads I'm pretty hungry aye.' 'OPc you are fat cunt haha.' My cousins laughed. Joey told me there was some hot food on the table inside. Without hesitation I wipped myself a new hot plate and munched away. 'Fach this shit is bussin.'

Eating away, my addays pulled up to the kitchen. 'KEFE, aikue, aua le ai he meai ole faifeau, sau ii.' Slap, bam, two hard hits landed on my face. I dropped the plate, and gapped back to the garage. All my siblings and cousins bursted out laughing, 'Haha, shame cunt, you thought.' 'Fuck all yous ya'll sad.'

I'd just finish doing my maths home work, I went to my room double sided bed with big comfy blankets etc. Settled down at my budget gaming set up, turnt on my gaming monitor and Ps4. I grabbed my NBA 2K21 disc and loaded it up to the main screen, I lost the case for it but I couldn't replace it with a new one because it was expensive. The game had just notified me a 1 million credit was sent to my gaming account, in that moment I felt so rich but it wasn't a rich in reality. I knew by the look of my room I was still in the reality of the poor life.

Poor Words

low life dog
broke cunt
povo the gronk
junkie dog
rachet cunt
poor fucking dog
retarded junkie

> scabing cunt
> hori cunt
> scumbag
> crach head
> druggo
> ai kupe
> retarded flop

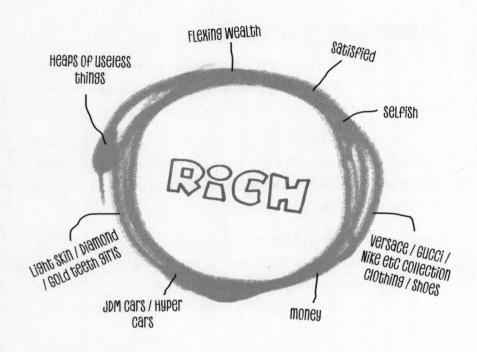

RiCH

Flexing wealth

Satisfied

Selfish

Versace / Gucci / Nike etc collection clothing / shoes

Money

JDM Cars / Hyper Cars

Light Skin / Diamond / Gold teeth girls

Heaps of useless things

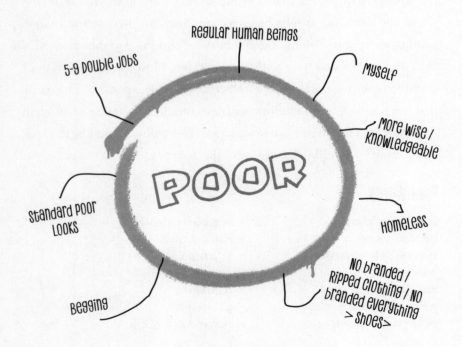

POOR

Regular Human Beings

Myself

More wise / Knowledgeable

Homeless

No branded / Ripped clothing / No branded everything > shoes>

Begging

Standard Poor Looks

5-9 Double Jobs

Untitled & Anonymous

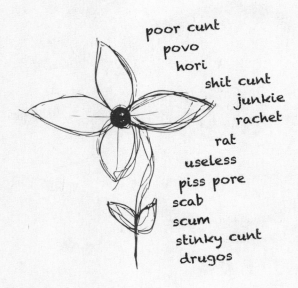

poor cunt
povo
hori
shit cunt
junkie
rachet
rat
useless
piss pore
scab
scum
stinky cunt
drugos

1. When I didn't have a job, 3 children & only had one income we didn't have enough money to pay the electricity bill, water bill, mortgage and put food on the table every week.

2. It was hard when we struggled to pay for the kids school stuff & having to explain we don't have enough money.

3. When I didn't have a job and 3 children and one income we didn't have enough money to get by then I went Tafe did some study in a job I wanted to do, found a job & started making more money, now this yr I can rebuild my home.

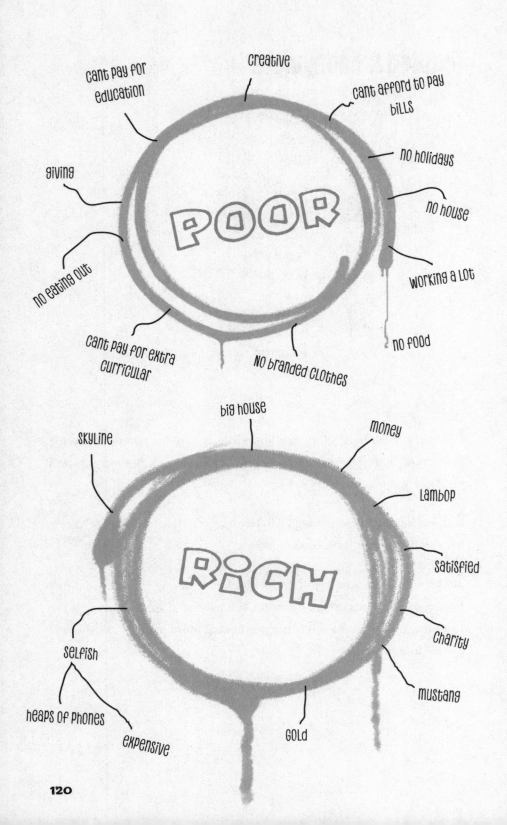

Crumbs

Edited by Sara M. Saleh

The Bus

Fahad Ali

The air was ripe with noise: parents chattering, engines humming, and children calling out to one another, punctuated every so often by the impatient yelp of a car horn. Hussain walked out the school gates with a heavy backpack in tow and made for the bus stop across the road. A river of cars moving stop-start down the street separated him from his destination.

A swarm of students had already assembled at the stop. Hussain joined them. Before long, the bus appeared in the distance, but it didn't slow down as it approached. As it rolled past, Hussain saw the driver — a usually expressionless man with a shiny, bald head — turning his face towards the window with a knowing smile and wave to the crowd.

Perhaps it was understandable. The day before, some of the more boisterous boys, a mess of untucked shirts and stringy limbs, had taken it on themselves to announce that various people on the bus were wankers. 'Jacob's a wanker,' they chanted in unison, clapping or drumming along to the rhythm. Once they were assured that Jacob got the point, they bestowed the title on someone else. 'Can you guys just stop?' pleaded Sophie. 'Sophie's a wanker,' they agreed. Sophie slunk back into her seat, defeated, and endured a few rounds of chanting. Suddenly, there was a pause. It was someone else's turn to cop it, but the boys seemed to have exhausted all possible options. Then: 'The driver's a wanker.' They continued chanting before the driver realised. With his face twisting into rage and his bald head crowned with sweat, he stopped the bus and fired off some expletives in the general direction of the passengers.

The driver had not forgotten. A roar of outrage came from the crowd as the bus passed them by. The crowd began to disperse. Hussain had to decide: would he wait for the next bus, or walk?

Theotokos

Nadia Demas

I watched you, quietly, from the bottom of a suitcase filled with hope as you fled the land I'd once fled to. You wanted to escape poverty and persecution, and no one could begrudge you. You carried me close and prayed my intercessions would carry you here. Then curiously, I sat over the kitchen-living-dining room, but who wouldn't seek out refuge for their children? You prayed their faith would grow in a chapel carved whole from Port Said and planted into hostile bushland, surrounded by trees foreign and bare. Now mute, behind a glass pane, حنوط taped to my spine, as the suburbs grew safer and echoes prayed silent. You prayed for better schools, better children, a better income. Mothers always want the best for our children.

You had a vision of your daughter; preacher, father, thriving where you toiled. You were prophetic, knew her better than he knew himself. You saw the best of what you wanted in her. But I was the one left to watch the border door and the despair that grew behind it. I attended silently as your shameless thorns of criticism grew. She prayed Ava Theotokos just as you had, begging to be seen. You bore that guilt, stated it with unspoken apologies, and I beamed in the evening light. I watched as the space between two rooms grew impenetrable with tensions. Your praise would not reach the threshold. What could I do but watch? Would that I had a mouth to speak or that you had ears to hear. Mothers always hope a glare will suffice.

I watched you, as you wove words from the Agpeya over the dreams that you laid that night. And those words for health came measured like a tithe. We both lost a son; your child still lives. But what is her health against your dignity? The حنوط at my spine, reserved for revered dead saints, sits waiting. No mother passes without sin, or is beyond forgiveness. And what choice do I have but to watch for redemption?

The Guy with the AMG

Jenanne Ibrahim

Peer beneath the surface, be heedful and wise,
As society will have you envy poverty's luxurious disguise.

The blinker ticks and ticks as they wait on the driveway of Centrelink Bankstown. Countless vehicles whoosh by: four-wheel drives packed with school kids, HiLuxes carrying tired tradies, teens in Corollas gobbling on their Macca's meals. Osman sits in the passenger seat, his mother sighing behind the steering wheel as they face the endless motorcade of the after-school run. Since they're in a run-down 2003 Toyota Camry, Osman buries his face into his shoulder to hide from his school friends who are always hanging around Bankstown.

Tick, tick, tick — they finally get a break and slide within the trail of cars on Meredith Street. Off they go, the Camry's brakes squeaking as they near every red light. Osman slumps his head further into his shoulder. His mother sighs. 'Don't worry, Osman, one day you will be a successful man and drive your dream car,' she says.

Osman looks up at his mother, his mouth downturned as he remembers how hard she works, how little she sleeps and how rough it's been ever since his father left. But then, his head snaps back to the road. His eyes catch the glimmer of a glossy black masterpiece that shines in the sun. The smooth, sloping roofline seamlessly shimmers, a fine coupe in all its glory with an aggressive Pan Americana grille, an elegantly monstrous vehicle.

Osman stares, his face bright as he witnesses his dream car manoeuvring the road before him with graceful finesse. The car he and his friends rave on about every lunchtime. The Mercedes C63s AMG. Who is driving and how can they afford it?

His mother catches his wonderment. 'It looks like they're going the same way as us,' she points out, every turn identical to theirs.

Eventually, they end up in their street. The AMG driver pulls into the driveway of an old fibro shack, its paint peeling and walls crumbling. Osman stares wide-eyed and perplexed. 'But, how? That car is $230k!' he exclaims.

The driver steps out of his vehicle, clad in a golden Versace jumper. He walks over to his front door and pulls out his keys.

'Ah yes. Isn't it typical, Osman?' his mother says. 'The poor guy who wears big brands and drives a flashy car to impress others but can't actually afford that lavish lifestyle. I betchya he can't keep up with the car repayments. Your father is just like him.'

The Daktor

Leila Mansour

Rumours of the Daktor's visits travel fast in Tareka. They always seem to coincide with school holidays on this side of the Mediterranean; which also coincide with waves of seasonal flus in winter and heat strokes in summer. Lucky for us, the Daktor's visits come when his services are most needed.

It is never said outright; sometimes hinted at in conversations at the breakfast table, between sips of coffee and bites of manakish. Khalto Salwa would say, 'The lights were on near the old butchery yesterday', and we always understand. The Daktor is visiting.

You see, the Daktor doesn't come down to Tareka anymore. Not since he bought the land near Abu Emad's butchery where rusty hooks still hang behind a frosty windowpane, though no meat has hung on those hooks in sixteen years.

The Daktor doesn't come down to Tareka anymore. Not since the classmates he used to roll marbles with on the cracked gravel of the local school yard have painted the last wall of his new house. We bet the Daktor felt generous at the thought of hiring the old friends who never made it as far as he did.

It doesn't matter that the little corner store on the main street still sells the cans of tamarind he drank more than water as a teenager. Hajjeh Em Rabeeh, who was his mother's neighbour for forty-three years, still remembers the mischief he and his cousins used to plot to get a taste of her fig trees before they'd even ripen. The Daktor just doesn't come down to Tareka anymore. It is us who go to him.

We admit, we don't visit the Daktor for the sake of visiting. He is under no illusions but he likes to play 'the prodigal son returned' and we in turn like to spare ourselves a hefty medical bill.

We ask him about our joint pains and the occasional tummy ache while eyeing pictures framed and hung on the wall of his blonde wife on their wedding day — the blonde wife who has never come out to greet us.

He tells us about his life on the other side of the Mediterranean. He calls it home and makes references none of us understand in foreign syllables we never thought the tongue of a Lebanese boy could mellow enough to enunciate.

There is always a pinch when he calls over there, home. We thought here is his home. But we understand. We would have left Lebanon too if we could.

Mealtime

Priyanka Bromhead

She tried to stay focused as her neighbour pointed to the large Tupperware container in the bottom of the fridge.

'He won't eat this cold, so make sure you take it out and leave it on the bench an hour before his mealtime, so it drops to room temperature. Use that chopping board, that's Milos' one specifically, you see the paws on it? Cute, no? I got it engraved especially for him when we were in the Hunter. Have you been? Oh, of course, you're not old enough for that kind of thing.'

She extended a papery-arm. Her hand clutched a small bottle with a vet's logo sprawled across it. Not the local one, but one a good thirty minutes or so from here, in the inner west, where the streets, like inner-west-vellais' minds, were dusty, narrow and hard to get through. Only the best vet for the little furball.

'Crush one of these in with his loaf once it's at room temperature and then add about a hundred grams of the steak on top.'

Steak.

Hers was a beef-free home, despite not being a Hindu one. Ammamma grew up in a convent school but still held Śaiva traditions close. On Fridays they were a veg home but every other day was a non-veg day. Their two-bedroom flat was full of the smells of sāmbarani, fried melahai and Dettol. But never beef. What would that even smell like? And could she feed a dog The Holy Cow? She'd have to check with Amma.

She nodded politely and repeated back the instructions like she was made to in the ESL class she wasn't supposed to be in. She waited awkwardly by the French provincial furniture, not wanting to touch or break anything, while Mrs. Margaret Mather (nee Ponniah, of Cinnamon Gardens) loaded her olive-green Benz and left for the third time in as many months.

Hours later, she made her way to the kitchen; small, neat, organised, and prepared Milos' meal. She remembered that for dinner, Amma was making tinned-fish curry, syrupy in its tomato-chilli flavours and silky in the way that it fell apart if you meddled with it too much.

She slipped a small gelatinous piece of the loaf into the bowl, and a piece in her own mouth.

Chicken, rice and vegetables. The label said $16.99.

Crushed the tablet. $43.98.

Steak slice, bowl loaded, she watched in envy at Milos. The overgrown rat ate better than she ever had.

Skittles and Rice

Helen Nguyen

The warm grains made the lollies shed their bright and hard shells. Ong Ngoai stood in a moss-coloured sweater in our paint-chipped kitchen, stirring the skittles into the rice with metal chopsticks. Winter light flooded into the house through cheap lace curtains. I ate my lunch on a red plastic chair by Ba Ngoai's feet. Her dialysis machine sat beside her massage chair — tied to her like a dog on a leash. Ba Ngoai's bob of white hair floated around her wrinkled face like a bowl of hot congee. She coloured Bratz colouring books with me, purply fingers gripping the Faber-Castell pencils.

'Ba Ngoai!' I groaned, the Smurf stain of blue skittles on my lips. 'You don't colour in their face, they are not Shreks.'

Ba Ngoai slumped back into her maroon chair. 'Do it yourself then,' she said. My mouth dropped open. Ba Ngoai was my friend. I played all my activities with her; most of them sitting down because she was very sick. One afternoon, we played Hide & Seek. I hid behind her dialysis machine, my butterfly clips sticking out behind the plastic hose. In this game, I only hid within a few metres from Ba Ngoai's massage chair, so she could pretend to find me without needing to stand up. If she stopped entertaining me, I had no one else to play with.

We lived in a one-storey unit in West Sunshine with a terracotta roof and burnt dirt backyard. We hung our floral bed sheets and stained white socks on a sagging metal clothesline above the earth. In the dim, grainy-tiled kitchen, behind jars of Chinese medicine, canned spam and tubs of rice, was a lilac rice cooker. The house smelt of cooked rice, tiger balm, and incense. Life was the colour of cha lua. My dad, a boat refugee from Vietnam, worked seven days a week at Bunnings after graduating from Melbourne University with a Bachelor of Engineering. My mum, a sponsored migrant, was working at the bank. I saw them as little as I saw fresh plums in our kitchen.

Ba Ngoai and I had to get creative. While my parents were away building a stable life for us, we played dress-up with our food — conning our way to the luxury life with the food colouring of Skittles. When I stuck out my blue tongue, it looked as though I had just swallowed a fresh punnet of blueberries.

—

The summer I turned twelve, Ong Ngoai and Ba Ngoai passed away. Mum started cooking for me. My lunch and dinner now had variety: sunny banh xeo overfilling with leafy bean sprouts, prawn ball soup full of lettuce and mint and chilli-speckled chicken pho. As my diet grew, so did my father's career. He secured more electrical engineering contracts, often for three to six months in places like Bendigo, Auburn or Ballarat. As he earned more, my mother went part-time at the bank and then quit entirely.

'You are growing up now,' she said to me in our sagging kitchen that smelt of boiled barramundi and bleach. 'You need to eat. Good food for good brains. We only got once-chance when we in Year 12, we must do well for Ong Ba. Cannot disappoint them.' I believed my mum regretted her absence in my early childhood, almost as much as she regretted not being there for the last years of Ong Ngoai and Ba Ngoai's life. This was her redemption. Each longan she cracked open for me was like a plea for forgiveness, sugar juice dripping down her bony elbows.

One evening, she snuck out of our joint three-person bedroom to use the bathroom. I saw her kneeling on the tiles before our shrine, praying to the framed photographs of Ong Ngoai and Ba Ngoai. 'Forgive me Ba Me. Forgive me for making you eat that crap while I was always gone.' Tears slid down her cheeks. She was feeding me more and more and I was getting chubbier — but Mum herself slimmed. I watched her weeping then went back to our room to sleep.

The year after, I started at a private girl school in Toorak. We moved out of the two-bedroom unit in West Melbourne to a modern, double-storey house in Cairnlea. The kitchen bench was made of glistening marble. Our new fridge, three thousand dollars from Footscray Bing Lee, cracked filtered water into ice. Its radiant shelves held boxes of soy milk and fresh paper-wrapped salmon. Behind a pearly vase of fresh orchids, our matte black Tiger rice cooker exhaled dragon puffs of quinoa-smelling steam.

One evening, I pulled open the pantry, lonely for artificial colour, and found only roasted almonds.

Our dinners were now homemade and had various proteins. Starting with soup, mien ga or canh cai. Followed by lemon-baked barramundi, lemongrass beef stir fry or sticky pork with fried egg. For dessert, my mum made lotus seed che and red coconut soi. Every meal was brought before the shrine that encased framed photographs of Ong Ngoai and Ba Ngoai, with an incense lit so my ancestors could return home to eat with us. Once, they had all been squeezed into housing commission, fighting for canned spam with yelling that echoed onto the grim streets of Flemington. Now, crab noodles overflowed from bowls.

I finished dinner with my Loreto Mandeville Hall skirt bursting at my waist. My mother stood above the white ribbon in my hair wearing silk pyjamas and peeling a papaya. 'Have a second breath,' she said. 'Then, we will eat some more.'

The glossy red packet leapt out at me from the confectionary aisle at Pitt Street Woolworths Metro. I was hurrying back to the office to finish affidavits, brown rice and salmon supermarket sushi in hand. I came to a halt. A packet of Skittles. The past few years as a law student reduced my existence into a blur of Soul Origin salad, morning spin class, and applying mascara on the bus. Most evenings, I wrestled myself on the elliptical at 8pm after work, especially if I ate too many Tim Tams from the office cookie jar.

Now, I stood staring at my childhood through a rainbow portal. I wept, thinking about how my grandparents were not alive to witness the luscious food my mother made to compensate for our once-poverty — seeking forgiveness. Since when did I start thinking all the protein and salad and avocado was a given? My Fitbit flashed. 1:03pm. I hugged the packet of Skittles into my chest and hurried to the International section to buy a packet of microwave jasmine rice.

In the office, waiting by the humming microwave, I grinned. Smashing the Skittles into the heated rice, I watched the hard shells bleed and swirl artificial colours through the steaming grain. At once a kid again and never quite an adult. I sent a selfie to my mum. My eyes moon-shaped with happiness. She responded instantly. 'Why you eating that stuff and get fat? I sent you money to buy barramundi.'

Ecologically Sustainable Household

Yasir Elgamil

40 at the end of the street was always cold. The cold in the house had a personal vendetta against my parents, sister and I. The way it dried our skin, ached our bones and stung our nostrils every time we breathed in. The settling of dust was unrelenting, immediately rushing onto any space one of us had just cleaned. Grout occupied the space between tiles and mould blackened the walls, and although invisible, we knew its fungal spores danced in the air and made themselves into our lungs. The house was just as much a victim to the elements as us. Its frail and wooden skeleton threatened to collapse each time the fat brushtail possum, which lived in our roof, pattered heavily around at night. I imagined it was cosier up there than we were below. The house had glass eyes that glazed over with filthy condensation like cataracts. The paint on the walls peeled off like eczema.

It's not that we neglected the house. Asking for assistance from our housing commission was out of the question. Our landlord would consistently warn against it in an annoyed mumbled ramble with the words, 'Trouble', 'Expensive' and 'Hassle' always strewn about. Then came his assurances that he'd fix the issues, delivered with a gummy smile and the same tone adults use when giving empty promises to children. Eventually, sketchy third-party workers he hired would trot in begrudgingly to fix minor issues, responding only in grunts and labouring in a rush. Like a toxic relationship, they were just plastering band aids over a house drowning in its own blood. When the workers removed the mould, the colours of the walls were so striking it felt like we had been viewing life through a monochromatic greyness. But inevitably, the mould returned and smothered everything into dullness once again.

You could say we were an ecologically sustainable household. My mother would read our monthly electricity, water and gas usage rates like a sports analyst breaking down a team's stats on ESPN. 'The Adarob family are extremely efficient, with combined usage less than that of the average Australian individual!' At such good news she would hold the paper bills to her chest and a proud smile would emanate through her eyes. 'However, their heat usage rates have increased significantly compared to last month.' At the mention of such discrepancies, she would target individuals. 'Samar, I've told you a million times that light you leave on in your room is wasting energy!'

Samar, my little sister, would scrunch her small nose aggressively. Her narrow eyes flickered with victimhood, in protest to being targeted. However, she held her tongue because she knew she was the undefeated champ of energy expenditure in the household.

'And Ibraheem,' my mother continued, 'I told you to cut out the hot water when washing the dishes, it's hardly necessary!'

Ibraheem, my father, would slightly purse his lips out in annoyance; a habit of his whenever he felt unfairly criticised. We called it the duck face.

Protecting ourselves from the cold was a part of everyday life, like opening the fridge or using the bathroom. Our pyjamas consisted of layers: t-shirts, sweaters, gloves, beanies, winter socks. To complete the ensemble, thick bathrobes my mother had bought for us were worn for everything except their intended use. Even after my sister and I abandoned them for more conventional clothing, my mother refused to abandon hers, continuing to don it in all its aged purple elegance. And in the case of my father, outerwear was innerwear. He would move around the house in his tanned nubuck jacket that always exaggerated his narrow shoulders, making him resemble a very large man.

In the coldest months, when we shuffled around the house dressed like Kathmandu mannequins, we'd beg Mother if we could turn on the air con, hot vapour escaping our mouths. 'No. Albas tageel. Wear something heavy,' she'd reply with a tone of finality, without looking up from her book. Our air con was a lonely machine, idling in neglect on our living room wall for years, except for the fleeting moments guests visited.

When the front door knocked, my mother would halt whatever she was doing and fumble with the air con remote to turn on the heat. Today, it was Amo Abbas, a tall man with a large dark beard that distracted from the light brown baldness of his head. My mother opened the door smiling so hard her eyes squinted. Then, after ushering Amo Abbas to the couch, Mother retreated into the kitchen to prepare offerings for our newly arrived guest.

Amo Abbas, sinking into the leather, humbly yelled out to my mother to not burden herself with anything. 'No need to make anything, Suraya. You know I'm just stopping by before I go to security!' Our house was on the way to his work. My mother yelled back, 'Chai bas, Allek Allah!' Amo heartily chuckled as he yielded to the unrelenting Sudani hospitality.

After exchanging last minute humorous quips as they farewelled each other, Mother immediately turned off the air con. The instant Samar heard the thud of the front door close, her curly mane appeared from behind her bedroom door — taking in the aftermath of the visit with suspicious eyes. Tea and assorted biscuits sitting on ornate trays made the warmth of the living room palpable. Usually, Samar would disappear back into her lair after passing silent judgement, but this time she'd had enough. 'Oh, I see how it is!' My mother stared at her daughter blankly. The cheeriness from a few minutes ago had completely dissipated. 'So they get the air con, but we're supposed to walk around the house freezing to death like it's *Man vs. Wild*?'

Life in 40 was like a sitcom. All that was missing was the laugh track.

Sand Paradise

Jessicca Wendy Mensah

From Liverpool through Kensington

to Gold Coast, a refined sand city.

I counted veins and arteries,

then I couldn't find mine.

Today my neighbour surfed.

Yesterday he had coffee at Palm Beach,

the paradise of British 'G'day!'

I'm invisible like air, yet needed

like the evening sky, I'm black

with white stars surrounding me,

shining through my overnight shifts

hoping the sun doesn't shine.

My vein is below the dark,

I'm a citizen of the sky,

questioned about my afro.

I am Australian.

The Song that Fills the Valley

Katie Shammas

'Wa habibi wa habibi, aya hali anta fih?' There is singing through the wadi where the wheat grows and the dates are harvested. The same song echoes through the bush from the house Dad built as silver sun shines through the dancing rain.

There are six around the kitchen bench. Mum wakes first, wrapped in her velvety emerald robe. Followed shortly by Dad, who holds Hawa, my sister, snuggled in the warmth of his blue check pyjamas. She rubs sleep from her black eyes with a small pudgy fist. I emerge next, waltzing down the stairs from side to side, followed by my older sister, Mariam; her olive skin still dewy from the shower. Last to emerge is our only brother, Usef, who greets us with a grunt, having slept in after a late night.

On the kitchen bench, instead of toast and labne is an aqua green plastic bowl of semolina pastry, a smaller bowl of spiced minced dates, and a collection of shiny steel pastry ma'alet. The kitchen smells of butter and cloves. We stay in our pyjamas till lunchtime and our humming fades then escalates as we fight to be heard. We are making kaek.

Hawa's small hands rhythmically roll out the date mix into long thin snakes. Usef helps her but mostly watches. Mariam, the eldest, is the only one trusted to roll out the pastry, stuff it with the date snakes and circle it into a crown. I use the mal'at to decorate each kaek round with thorns. Mum says our work is almost as good as our paternal teta and how she wished we tried her infamous kaek.

Dad's job is to find the cassette that hides the voice of Fairuz like a secret in its thin, magnetic ribbon. He loops around us slowly and then pauses to take up a mal'at. All the while he sings along with the famous soprano. He only sings when we are together, his voice low and mournful like a magpie warble. Mum tells him off because his kaek are a creative mess stuffed too heavy with dates. They are delicious to eat, but no amount of icing sugar could make them fit to present to guests.

While we bake, Fairuz's voice unravels from the spool of tape. Each kaek round we make is delicate and trembling like the song. 'Wa habibi wa habibi, aya hali anta fih?'

Dad's calloused hands are buried deep in the silent earth. It has been eight months. Drawers have been emptied and cassettes piled on the floor as we look for the one that holds the song that filled the valley. The lonely wail of a black cockatoo echoes through the bush. I never want to make kaek again.

But, like the harvest of wheat and dates in the land we lost, rituals demand attention. Mum wears Dad's blue check pyjama shirt beneath her emerald robe. She gathers her now adult children and submerges her large soft hands into the semolina and butter.

Dad's clothes still hang in the wardrobe — the scent of Aramis and its notes of myrrh and clove fading. His office is a place no one dares enter: shelves and drawers quiet with the building plans that seized the blood in his heart. Usef, brave and alone, searches through Dad's things. Amongst old letters and unpaid bills, my brother finds the old cassette.

There are five around the kitchen bench. Silent, we make tray after tray of kaek. Mum looks at me when I make fat ones especially for Dad — but says nothing. My sisters work quietly and my brother paces. The breaths between Fairuz's call and the choir's response sit heavy in the air like soil turned to mud in the rain. 'Wa habibi wa habibi , aya hali anta fih?'

My mum tells us a story. She was still living in Abu Hanna's place in the small Galilean village she sought refuge in with her parents when she was a baby. The house was now too full and noisy with all her siblings and Abu Hanna's family. It was the wheat harvest and though she enjoyed the thousand and one tales told by the elders, she was counting the days. At the end of summer, she was going to Haifa to become a nurse.

There is a faint trill in Mum's voice as she tells us it was at that time when she and Dad noticed each other on the Haifa beach. She was on a break with a nursing friend eating pastries and he was playing volleyball. They smiled at one another, recognising they were from the same village. But there was something more. Mum says she felt the rumble of a choir in her chest.

Months passed and Mum returned home the week where the lamentation for those who lost everything is sung every night and the villagers fill the streets with olive branches and palms. Mum and Dad saw each other again in the singing crowd. Later she was with her sisters and the other women of the house making kaek. Dad came by to speak with her and her father.

We listen carefully to the tale we've heard many times. Together, with our fingers pressed in pastry, the stories of wheat and dates and land and ancestors are summoned around our kitchen bench.

In the very last song on the cassette, Fairuz and her choir call to one another like lorikeets welcoming a new day. It used to be my least favourite, especially during the years it was just the five of us. Dad's voice was silent and in that song I heard the story of him and Mum — two young people who left a stolen homeland for a dream that beckoned them but never came true.

We bake with six again when my daughter, the first grandchild, is born. Elene wakes beside me, warm and smelling of milk. I carry her down the stairs Dad built. Mum clucks and coos, quickly washing her hands from pastry to sweep Elene up into the embrace of her emerald robe. Mariam, Hawa and Usef circle around us singing a lilting chorus to make their niece smile.

One by one more babies are born, bringing the abundance of a returned homeland full of the noisy love of ancestors and family. We don't need the cassette anymore. It is packed away with Dad's blue check pyjamas, letters and building plans. Fairuz's lamentations and my father's passion are now on Spotify. Usef, the brave father of three noisy wild sons, connects his phone to the speakers. His eldest Nakhli, my father's namesake, is the first in the kitchen to help his teta.

With everyone's new partners, lovers, kids and friends, there are eighteen around the kitchen bench. My mother wears the same emerald robe. Bowls of semolina pastry, spiced dates and the same shiny ma'alet are spread across the bench. The same smell of butter and cloves fills the air, mixing with our frustrated yells as we try to control the children.

In moments of silence, we hear Fairuz's finale summoning new life. Mum remarks that my daughter's decorations are delicate like my grandmother's. And my nephew makes big fat unruly ones like my father.

There is singing through the wadi, where the wheat grows and the dates are harvested. The same song echoes through the bush from the house Dad built as silver sun shines through the dancing rain. 'Wa habibi wa habibi, aya hali anta fih?'

Some of the Sun

Phoebe Grainer

It has become an everyday thing for me to stand under the burning star every morning. I have been sad and out lately and I heard light was supposed to make you feel better. It's stinking hot out, heat warming up skin like fire cooking some poor sweet river fish — but I don't want to move. I stretch my hands out in front of me and try to hold the sun, it casts shadows on my body. But in my hands, it strikes shiny glowing light. If I could hold the sun, maybe I could swallow it. Swallow it so it could light up and spread its glow in the dark storm in my belly.

'Lea!' Mum yells out through the kitchen window. I barely make out her soft chestnut face behind the window screen. 'Come and have mayi!' I grab my working boots and take a bit of the sun, gently put the glow in my pocket and walk inside.

'Don't forget a hat, it's hot out there.' Dad sits at our family table, brown eyes look down behind his big glasses, reading the *Queensland Register* that has cattle on the front page. He takes a sip of his McDonald's flat white. 'And your water. What time you coming home?' Mum bites into her buttered white toast in the tiny square kitchen. She offers me a slice and pushes a cuppa in my direction, I grab it. 'I don't know.' I dip my white toast into the tea.

Mum reminds me of that tea — caramel and dark creamy. Me, I'm more like black tea.

I take another mouthful and look at Mum and Dad. Dad still reading and Mum looking towards the TV. Mum and Dad are like the sun. The pale weather man talks about extreme weather conditions. Everyone says I look like Mum. Mum's eyes are darker than Dad's. Her eyes shine like the black rocks in the river around our town. I drink the rest of my tea and wash my cup. Mum stares at me with those shiny black eyes. 'And don't forget to ask him how much you getting paid.'

'Junga please,' Dad says, looking up at me smiling. He rubs his thumb and index fingers making the money sign.

I laugh and shove the white toast in my mouth, it scratches and dries my throat. A thunder vibrates in my stomach. *I need all the money I can get if I'm gonna get out of this town and follow the sun.* 'Come on,' Dad eggs me on, always wanting to make me laugh.

I go to the oven and take out my bacon and egg toastie that I'm gonna eat for smoko and I wrap it in foil and put it into my bag. 'If it's too hot, tell them to bring you home. Didn't them mob die out there last year?' Dad says and looks at Mum, his hairy eyebrows raised behind his glasses. 'Hmm hmph. One from the heat and the other from a snake bite,' Mum adds. She takes another bite of her white toast.

Pepper, Benji and Oli start barking and there are two horn beeps. 'There, quick. They're there now!' Mum and Dad yell at me, turning their heads towards the noise.

I get my lunch. Rice, beef stew, soft drink, boiled eggs and an orange. The screen door slams on my way out. Oli follows me, barking at the white bus with white rims. *Why is everything always white?* Oli jumps on my shin and bounces back on the ground. 'See ya, buddy.'

I close the iron gate and run out past the palm trees and onto the big white bus with 'Tonganado' and a tornado printed in black on the side. I smile and the sun in my pocket smiles too. *These fullas true.* Sione is in the front seat. 'Morning.' Big twenty-dollar service station sunglasses and white and gold teeth gleam back at me. There is another big Tongan man next to him. He's burnt orange and looks like that shark alien from *Lilo & Stitch*.

The seats are empty except for an Italian fulla with fat lips. I wonder if someone was Black in his family way back when. I sit behind him. 'Hey.' He barely moves his mouth.

'Morning.' The Tonganado sets off, leaving a swirling ruby cloud. 'What's your name?' Fat Lip looks at me with his gecko eyes.

'Lea.'

'Oh, I'm Leo.'

He must be a new Italian. The Italians from here own the farms not work on them. 'What farm we going?' I ask him and pray it's not bloody mangoes or banana.

'Grape.' Fat Lip turns and puts his earphones on. Techno beats. Typical backpacker music.

We stop at the old caravan park and heaps more backpackers jump in. I don't even need to hear them speak to know they're not from here. The way they walk, hold themselves, their clothes, their laugh. They're different to the people in town. I wonder what makes them stand so upright. *Is it the sun?*

There is a group of French men. They take a seat at the front near the shark alien. They talk loud and fast to each other. I think about Dad and Mum at home and wonder what it would be like if we could speak our language loud and fluently like them. I start saying all the language words I know in my head. I count to fifteen before we stop on the side of the main street near an old wooden Queenslander, it's painted yellow. Some Indonesians come on, there are more women than men, all covered with sun protection. The girls have sun masks over their hijabs. They're gonna be so hot out there with this sky today.

The sun-smart Indonesians sit behind the loud French blokes and play on their cat cover iPhones. Everyone looks tired and buggered up.

I wonder if I look like that too. Looking at my reflection in the windows of the Tonganado. Country-coloured skin and river rock eyes like Mum. Then I look out past it. The town passes by. It's mostly brown, like the dust of the earth is trying to disintegrate the town slowly back to what it was. Coles. McDonald's. Centrelink.

Another thunder shakes my stomach. A cousin joins the black and white line of the tobacconist. I wave at him as if he can see me but more so just to do something: I've become aware that I'm the only one like me on the bus. The old Grahams Pub, where my grandad used to sit, goes past. The bank.

Thunder. The corner where all the old fullas stand and watch everyone. They used to sit before the council took their chairs away. Thunder. The bookstore, shoe shop, Red Rooster.

I close my eyes and I can still see the town. Lightning strikes hard in the angry black cloud in my stomach. It stings me across my body. I open my eyes and wander upward. Tonganado stops, ruby cloud wafting in the air.

The sky is bright and blue. Hot air balloons float in the sky and I imagine I am out there. Air flowing through my black hair, the sun in my belly. I'm floating somewhere, anywhere, but here. A Japanese couple jumps aboard, the boyfriend has long black dreadlocks that reminds me of Bob Marley and the girl looks the same. A group of Fijian men follow after. They look like a professional football team, tall and solid and all wearing blue rugby shorts. The Fijian football team move their big bodies through Tonganado, it rocks and sways. They sit right at the back, except one. He has an afro surrounding his head like a black halo and tattoos on his dark skin. He is the tallest and he sits on the other chair across from me. A thunder roars loudly but it's not mine. I turn to the rumble... it's his. I quickly look forward but I can still see him. He leans on the glass window of the Tonganado. His hair like a soft black pillow. I know that expression he has on his face. I know he wants to be floating away in the sky too.

The colours of the people on the bus remind me of the different shades of dark brown on my mother's cheek. She said our women get it sometimes when they're pregnant. A birthmark of mother mood, a mark of womanhood, from her having me. Mum the sun. I relax my shoulders and my eyes start to gently close.

I am swimming in the ocean, the calm cool current sparkles. It is night. I dive under the water and open my eyes. There are stars in the ocean too. I watch as they move across my arms. They light everything up and I swim back to the surface and breathe in the gold stardust.

'Hey.' Fat Lip nudges me on my elbow, his head tilting to the group gathered outside the Toganado. They stand in front of the lines and lines and lines and lines and lines and lines and lines and lines of grape vines. *Seriously*.

I wipe the dribble off my cheek and glance to where Black Halo sat. He's gone. I pick up my lunch bag and follow Fat Lip off the bus. Sione moves his thick sandy arms to wrap the grape vine around the wire. 'See, like that,' he says. 'Have fun.' He's looking at me like he wants to laugh. I nod as if I was there the whole time. The chubby Indonesian girl next to me yawns. 'Do you want to go back to sleep?' Sione asks her jokingly. She looks to Sione and then to the ground, then she giggles. 'Pick youse up seven o'clock tonight.' The group look at him quickly. Sione laughs and takes a bunch of grapes, he walks chewing, mouth open; his gold fillings on his front teeth glitter in the sun. I watch him as he gets into the Tonganado and drives off leaving a swirling ruby cloud.

I wipe my face with my arm, sweat pooling on the sleeve of Dad's fisherman shirt, and look at the rows and rows and rows and rows and rows and rows and rows and rows and rows and rows and rows and rows and rows and rows and rows of grape vines. *Serrriiiioooussslyyy*. It's stinking hot out here.

'We not really staying here until seven?' I ask Fat Lip, who has already started to make other friends. He shrugs and continues to talk ignoring me. *Typical.*

Thunder. 'You, you, you go over there.' It's Shark Alien, pointing at me, the sun-smart Indonesians, Fat Lip and Black Halo, showing us where to work. I quickly take one massive bite of my bacon and egg toastie, shove it into my bag and throw it on the pile of backpacks under the closest grape vine.

I feel like I'm not supposed to be out here. Thunder. Like I'm not supposed to be here working these rows and rows and rows and rows and rows and rows and rows and rows and rows and rows and rows and rows and rows of grape vine. I feel I'm different. Thunder growls.

The people who got jobs in town; they don't look like these people. Thunderous winds go wild. These people need this. Some need it to survive even. They come from far away. They can't get jobs in town. I look at everyone. The stormy wind blowing in my belly. They've come seeking something. All different colours. All different faces. Seeking something. I'm not different. Thunder vibrates throughout my body. Seeking something to help them. The dark storm in my stomach swirls around like ruby dust from the Tonganado. I don't look like these people and I don't look like the people in town with jobs too. Rain pours in my stomach. I need this too, to survive, even. Buckets and buckets and buckets of rain. They have all come seeking something. *Just a few weeks, I'll get my money and then I'm outta here.* The rain is so heavy. There's so much rain. The rain is drowning me. *Maybe we all need the sun?*

I take out the sun I had taken this morning and I swallow some. 'We start?' a soft deep voice says to me. I look to the voice. Black Halo stands watching me. He looks stormy. The sun moves down into my black stomach. His dark chest rising and falling like a wave in his grey worn-out shirt. Everyone seeks something. The sun starts to shine some light. I hold my hand out and give him some of the sun.

More from Sweatshop

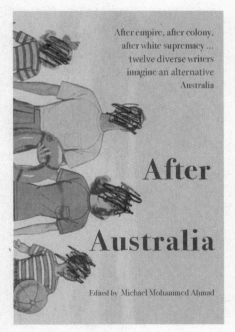

Sweatshop
Women

VOLUME ONE

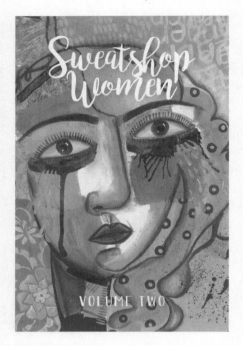

Sweatshop
Women

VOLUME TWO

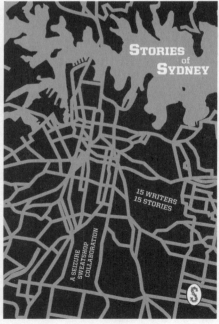

STORIES
of
SYDNEY

15 WRITERS
15 STORIES

A SEIZURE
SWEATSHOP
COLLABORATION

TAMAR
CHNORHOKIAN

The
DIET
STARTS ON
MONDAY

FINDING TRUE LOVE WILL TASTE SO SWEET

THE
BIG
BLACK
THING
CHAPTER. 1

THE
BIG
BLACK
THING
CHAPTER. 2

RACISM

Stories on fear, hate & bigotry

Edited by Winnie Dunn, Stephen Pham & Phoebe Grainer

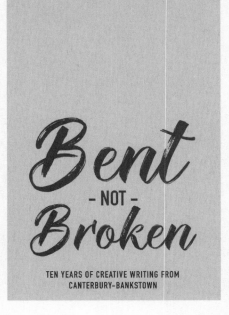

Bent
- NOT -
Broken

TEN YEARS OF CREATIVE WRITING FROM
CANTERBURY-BANKSTOWN